Happy Again!

Your New and Meaningful Life After Loss

HARRIET HODGSON

T0159284

Happy Again!
Your New and Meaningful
Life After Loss

HARRIET HODGSON

~By Harriet Hodgson
~Review by Dr. Heidi Horsley

Harriet Hodgson, the author of 30 books, is no stranger to overcoming adversity and finding happiness after loss. In her latest inspirational and moving book for all those who mourn, she asks, "Will I survive? Will I ever be happy again?"

After she was left to raise her twin grandchildren, while grieving for four family members, including her daughter, Harriet vowed not to let her deceased daughter down. Her pledge then and now: *Helen, I will not fail you.* Although Harriet has faced many challenges in her life, she describes multiple losses as the worst. Despite great adversity and loss, she reminds us that we are not alone in our grief, and, though losses may define our lives, they will not destroy them.

This book is a must-have for anyone who has lost a family member. Written in a conversational style, the chapters are a chronology of a grief journey, and the titles include:

- Life's New Roles
- The Impact of One Loss and Many
- Weaving Your Safety Net
- Unforeseen Challenges
- Tapping Your Inner Strength
- Self-Care Steps
- Affirming Yourself
- The Happiness Choice
- A New Normal, a New Life

Readers may turn to the resource section for more information, and there are blank pages for you to jot down your personal happiness plan. From start to finish, this book is all about help. In the preface Harriet tells how to make the most of *Happy Again!* and writes: *Think of this book as a happiness guide and the recovery tips as signposts. Like all signposts, you may follow them, ignore them, or return to them later. The choices you make depend on your needs, which change from day to day and, in the throes of early grief, from hour to hour. The suggestions in this book will help you plan the new life that awaits you.*

This book tugged at my heartstrings. Harriet's account of a journey from despair to hope is filled with practical suggestions on how to once again have a meaningful life. Her twin grandchildren were 15 years old when they moved in with her, and as the months passed, Harriet realized life had given her a choice. She could choose to be happy or choose to exist. Harriet is someone that has not only survived multiple losses, she has gone on to thrive. This book tells how she chose happiness, and gives you tools, tips, and sage advice for doing the same.

As the executive director for the Open to Hope Foundation, I highly recommend this book! Not only will I recommend it to bereaved families, I will recommend it to professionals and graduate students working in the field of grief and loss. *Happy Again! Your New and Meaningful Life After Loss* inspired me, and I think it will inspire you. ❖

Dr. Heidi Horsley, PsyD., is a bereaved sibling, as well as a psychologist. She is the executive director of the Open to Hope Foundation, cohost of the Open to Hope radio program, and an adjunct professor at Columbia University.

This book is published by the Centering Corporation, and can be ordered through their website at www.centering.org, or by calling 866-218-0101. Free shipping is offered to TCF chapters and members.

Published by WriteLife
(An imprint of Boutique of Quality Books Publishing Company)
www.writelife.com

in cooperation with

Grief Illustrated Press
PO Box 4600
Omaha, NE 68104
www.centering.org

Printed in the United States of America

Cover design by
Jay Highum, Rochester, Minnesota, USA

Cover Photograph © People Images, "Rain? Who Cares?!"

ISBN 978-1-60808-056-4 (p)
ISBN 978-1-60808-115-8 (e)

First Edition

TABLE OF CONTENTS

MAKING THE MOST OF THIS BOOK

The reading time for this book is about two and a half hours. You may read the chapters in any order. Where you begin depends on where you are in your grief journey. Before you start, grab a highlighter or colored pen to mark key points. Look for points that will help you create your personal happiness plan.

Think of this book as a happiness guide and the recovery tips as signposts. Like all signposts, you may follow them, ignore them, or return to them later. The choices you make depend on your needs, which change from day to day and, in the throes of early grief, from hour to hour. These suggestions will help you plan the new life that awaits you.

- Read the headings before you start a chapter.
- Highlight the points that "speak" to you.
- Use these points to start your new life plan on the blank page in the Appendix.

- Revise the plan as you go along.
- Read some of the books and articles cited in the resource list.
- Join a grief support group.
- Bring the book to support group meetings and discuss some of the topics it contains.
- Join a reliable online grief community.
- Set one or two new goals.
- Give a copy of *Happy Again!* to a bereaved relative or friend.
- Find something to be happy about each day.

PREFACE

"You look good," my friend said. We had met unexpectedly in the grocery store and stopped to chat. I was glad to see her because she is one of the few people who understand what I've been through. Despite the loss of her husband and two children, she is upbeat about life.

"Well, I uh . . . had my hair streaked," I replied.

"No, it's not that," she answered, studying me closely. "It's your face. You look happy – happier than I've seen you look in years." I am happy and have worked hard to get to this place in life.

In 2007 my daughter, father-in-law, brother, and former son-in-law died within nine months. My daughter and father-in-law died the same weekend. When I saw their photos on the same page of the newspaper my body shook with sobs. I have good coping skills and put them to use. But I would start to feel better and then another loved one would die. Though I've faced many life challenges, multiple losses were the worst, and life had never seemed so bleak. Looking in the mirror, I saw a sad, defeated woman, a woman totally without hope.

My daughter died in February from the injuries she received in a car crash. Our former son-in-law moved in with our twin grandchildren to care for them until they graduated from high school. Things were going pretty well until he died in November from the injuries he received in another car crash. It was unbelievable.

The twin's father was alive when the ambulance brought him to the hospital emergency room. He died about an hour later. Family members were numb with shock. We had just left the hospital and were standing on the sidewalk, when I turned to the twins and said, "You're coming home with us."

The instant I voiced these words, five little words, I knew life had changed forever. The twins moved a few feet away from me to talk, but I could hear bits of conversation. As usual, my grandson was protective of his sister. "Going home with grandma and grandpa makes sense," he soothed. "We've been having Sunday dinner with them for years and know the house."

His comment brought back happy and painful memories. On a balmy Sunday evening, as my daughter was backing out of our driveway, she stuck her head out of the driver's window and said, "I just made out a will. You and Dad are listed as guardians. Is this okay?"

"Sure," we called, never dreaming we would have to act on this clause. My daughter waved, the twins waved, and off they went. Now we were GRGs (grandparents raising grandchildren) and responsible for two stunned, devastated, vulnerable teenagers. Life had given us a new mission and it was sacred. Our pledge then and now: Helen, we will not fail you.

As days became weeks, weeks became months, and months became years, our admiration for the twins grew. Clearly, their parents had done an excellent job of preparing them for life. The twins were wary when they first moved in with us at age 15 ½, but they gradually learned to trust us and think of our home as theirs. Somehow, and I'm not quite sure how, we became a family.

In the early and middle stages of grief, when my feelings were raw, two questions haunted me: Will I survive this? Will I ever be happy again? You have probably asked yourself the same questions. Grief can't be rushed and finding the answers will take months. In my case, answering the questions took four years and lots of grief work.

Life has many unforeseen challenges. Thankfully, it has

unforeseen joys as well. Both of the twins graduated from high school with honors. The man our daughter planned to marry, a kind, caring, and brilliant person, stayed in touch with the twins and attended their graduation. He took a marvelous photo of the kids and we used it for a Christmas card. Every time I looked at the photo I cried. The question was, why? Finally, I realized the cause of my tears. For the first time, I saw hope in the twin's eyes.

Today, my grandson is attending a state university and is thinking of becoming a physician like his grandfather and great grandfather. My granddaughter is attending a small private college, majoring in public relations and art. She hasn't narrowed down her career choice yet, but is working on it. When the kids come home from college and walk in the door, they are smiling, eager, and excited about their lives.

The friend I met in the grocery store is right; I am happy. How did I find happiness? What steps did I take? Which ones worked best? The chapter titles are a chronology of my grief journey. Along the way, I realized life had given me a choice. I could choose to be happy or choose to exist. Of course, I chose happiness, and you can too.

Though you can't control life or death, you can control your responses to them. You are probably more resilient than you think and can "write" a good ending to your sad story. After all the sorrow, after all the tears, after all the pain, after all the worries, after all the challenges, happiness is a worthy goal. This book will help you reach it. You can be happy again!

1.
LIFE'S NEW ROLES

Life roles fall into two groups, new and established. The death of your loved one added a new role – mourner – to your list. You dreaded this role and now it has come to you. Worse, people are uncomfortable with the role, indeed, they are impatient, and expect you to recover in three months or so. Nobody can recover from loss in such a short time.

As I discovered, the mourner role has many painful sub-roles. For example, I wrote my daughter's obituary, my father-in-law's obituary (with input from relatives), and comments for our minister to read at our daughter's memorial service. Sitting at the computer, with tears running down my face, one sentence flashed in my mind again and again: *I can't believe I'm doing this.*

Hundreds of people came to our daughter's memorial service. The crowd was so large that many weren't able to sign the guest book. It didn't seem right to have a service for our daughter and not have a service for my father-in-law. But dad had asked us not to have a service and we honored his request. However, we showed his photo and noted his passing. Family members decided to hold a family memorial for him at a later date.

My husband and I had to find photos of our daughter for the photo presentation at the start of the service. We also had to choose a photo for cover of the service program. Years ago, our entire family, my husband and I, our two daughters, and the twins, went to the Isle of Man, the original home of the Hodgson family. We were fortunate to find a photo of our daughter and her children standing next to the Manx flag. The photo brought back many happy memories.

At our daughter's graveside, I spoke about the trip to the Isle of Man and how much it had meant to her. Three legs joined together in the middle are the symbol of the Isle and they represent the strength of the human spirit. The slogan explains the symbol: *Whichever way you throw me, I will stand.* In other words, we can triumph over life's adversities. Looking at the twins, I said, "This family loves you. This family cares for you. This family will stand."

MOURNER

Grieving for a loved one affects everything you do. The shock of loss may linger for a long time. You may dream about your loved one or have hallucinations. Many mourners become anxious and tense. It's hard to function when you have these feelings. Unpleasant images and memories may haunt you and, worse, you may fall into the "what if" trap.

In some cultures, mourners wear a special color or armband to tell others they are grieving. Many times I wished I had a lapel button that said, "Mourning. Please be kind." It would help others understand why I was confused, slow, short-tempered, or weeping. The symptoms of grief didn't shake my resolve. I had to be strong for my grandchildren and strong for myself.

Bob Deits, author of *Life After Loss: A Practical Guide to Renewing Your Life After Experiencing Major Loss*, thinks some key facts about mourning can actually be a foundation for recovery. Here are his facts, with some additional comments.

1. You can't avoid grief. The only way to deal with it is to accept the pain, or as Deits puts it, "go through it."

2. Though grief is a universal experience, your grief is the worst. You feel this way whether you have had one loss or several.

3. Grieving for a loved one is hard, exhausting work and there's lots of work to do. Just thinking about the work that awaits you is exhausting.

4. You can't accomplish your grief work without help from others. One friend can make all the difference. Several friends are an army of support.

"Learning to work with grief in these ways may feel strange and uncomfortable," Deits continues. "These ideas may represent a whole new way for you to think about grief." Grief takes time and taking the time you need is one of the best things you can do for yourself.

WIDOW/WIDOWER

Your new role may be that of a widow or widower, a role that sets you apart from others. Thankfully, I'm not a widow, but to understand the role, I interviewed several widowed friends. One was the widow of a physician. "What do you think of the word widow?" I asked.

"I don't like the word, but it's a fact," she answered. "That's how the public deals with you." She went on to say that being a widow wasn't her concept of self and didn't define her. "I'm not a lonely woman," she continued. "My children have been very supportive and I have good friends."

You may turn to family, friends and organizations for support if you are a widow or widower. AARP, the American Association of Retired Persons, has a variety of support services. Online support is available and there are widowed persons chapters all across the country. For more information go to the AARP website and enter the search words "widowed persons" or "grief and loss."

AARP has developed a "Guide for New Widows and Widowers," and it is available online. The guide makes some important points and one is about a myth. According to the myth, grief has an ending point and "if you just wait long enough" it goes away. This myth is false. "More than time, bereavement takes effort to heal," the guide explains. You'll really have to put forth some effort if you are a bereaved parent.

BEREAVED PARENT

My daughter was 45 years old when she died. She is gone forever and there is a large hole in my life. I will be a bereaved parent for the rest of my days. Still, I have the comfort of knowing my daughter lived long enough to see her twins become teenagers, earn an engineering degree, earn her MBA, supervise three production lines, and receive outstanding job reviews. During one of our last conversations, my daughter told me that she had been assured of advancement in the company.

She died just when she was soaring in life. Like all bereaved parents, I feel my child died too soon.

The death of one child is bad enough. A woman I know lost two adult children and I don't know how she copes. She is active in the community, shows up at events, smiles and jokes and makes witty comments, yet there is a sense of sorrow about her. I met her one day and asked automatically, "How are you?"

"Today is the anniversary of my daughter's death, so I'm not happy," she replied. "I swear a lot."

Bereaved parents need to be with understanding people. You may wish to join *The Compassionate Friends*, a national organization for those who have lost a child and their families. The organization has local chapters, holds yearly conferences, and publishes a magazine, "We Need Not Walk Alone." For more information please visit *www.compassionatefriends.org* or contact the national office at *nationaloffice@compassionatefriends.org*.

The *Open to Hope Foundation*, a non-profit group that provides online support for the bereaved, may also be a source of help. This website posts helpful articles from those who are grieving, grief experts and counselors. It also has a blog. Visit *www.opentohope.com* for more information.

SURVIVING SPOUSE

Surviving spouse may be your new role. Some mourners feel guilty about being a survivor. Richard Boyle addresses the survival issue in his article, "The Successful Survivor: The Widow's Journey." According to Boyle, widows and widowers can transition to a fulfilling life by addressing their emotions, taking care of their physical and financial health, and working towards a future.

This is easier said than done. Grief is exhausting and so are your new roles. You may have so many roles you can't keep track of them. At least, that is my experience. A small group of friends may become your support group.

If I go to the grocery store early in the morning, I see four or five widowers sitting at a table in the store restaurant. They have been meeting at the restaurant for years. When I go by, the men are having a serious discussion or laughing together. These surviving spouses have found a way to help each other and enjoy their lives. Talking with a surviving spouse may help you.

GRANDPARENT RAISING GRANDCHILDREN (GRG)

Weeks after our former son-in-law died, the court appointed us as the twin's guardians and conservators. My husband and I divided our duties. He handled estate matters and I handled household and school matters. Our legal roles ended when the twins turned 18 and we appeared in court for the ruling.

We were asked to come forward and sit at a table. Our lawyer made an opening statement and the judge read through the documents my husband had prepared. He didn't ask us to speak and, except for an occasional cough, the courtroom was quiet, too quiet, and I wondered if something was wrong. A few minutes later the he rescinded our guardianship and conservatorship. Then he looked at us and smiled. "Thank you for doing such a good job of raising your grandchildren," the judge said. His comment brought tears to my eyes.

Though the twins are in college now, we continue to be involved in their lives. We help with decision-making (when asked), homework (when asked), clothing choices (when asked), budgeting, estate management, income taxes and, most important, continue to provide a loving and nurturing home. Becoming GRGs has been one of the best experiences of our lives. My husband and I hope to be at the twin's college graduations.

SINGLE AND ALONE

Single may be your new role and it can be a surprising one. According to the physician's widow I interviewed, some female friends think she is after their husbands. "I'm not," she declared emphatically, "but these women have that little nagging feeling. It's usually younger women." Being single may end your contact with couple's groups. You may not participate in weekly bridge nights, for example, or couples' bowling.

Changes like these are hard to accept. In addition to losing a loved one, you have lost family structure, relationships, and connections. Like a boat breaking loose from its mooring, you have been cut loose, and may be drifting. The confusion and uncertainty of life make you feel alone.

The first two years the twins lived with us my husband and I felt alone and disconnected. We used to interact with other retired couples. After we switched to the high school schedule, however, we rarely saw these people. When we did see them, our conversations didn't mesh. Friends would talk about returning from Paris and we would talk about returning from Hy-Vee, the local grocery store. Our lives couldn't have been more different.

ADDITIONAL ROLES

Whether it's the single, GRG, surviving spouse, bereaved parent, widower, widow, or mourner role, these roles are in addition to the ones you already have. You may be the family provider, a family caregiver, or nurturer of adult children who have come back to live with you. How can you make sense of your roles? The Marshfield Clinic Education Foundation in Wisconsin has an article about sorting roles on its website. This article, "Multiple Roles," contains a short checklist.

Chances are you have some of the roles on it – son or daughter, brother or sister, aunt or uncle – and they take lots of time. Once you have identified your roles, the article says you should determine how much time you spend on each one. "Reduce your time in the least important roles," the article advises, and "be kind to yourself."

I had many roles: wife, physician's wife (a separate role), mother, grandmother, grandparent raising grandchildren, guardian, executor, driver, cook (a never-ending job), home manager, cleaning lady, committee chair, committee member, volunteer, club member, writer/author, website contributing author, and public speaker. My husband had just as many roles.

One role – substitute parent – was purposely omitted from our lists. We could never be substitutes for the twin's mother and father and wouldn't even try. "I hope you know we're not trying to replace your parents," I explained. "We're your grandparents and always will be." Though I can't prove it, I think the twins were glad to hear this.

Take a moment to think about your roles. How many do

you have? Which is the most important? Therese A. Rando, PhD, discusses roles in her book, *How to Go on Living When Someone You Love Dies*. "Changes from your past identity must be noted and grieved," Rando writes. In other words, you are capable of new roles and moving forward on the recovery path.

Taking on new roles helps you regain control over your life. As you assume these roles, Rando says you need to recognize the aspects of yourself that have remained constant, and there may be many. "This will provide you with a much needed sense of security and continuity," she explains. Though life has dealt you a terrible blow, it has also dealt new "cards" or options. One of your options is choosing new roles for your new life.

CHOOSING ROLES

Kristen Brooke Beck writes about changing roles in her article, "Life Roles." Some roles are permanent and some are temporary. Beck thinks conflicts arise when we have unwanted roles and cannot change them. "We can't control losing a loved one because we can't bring them back," she notes. This is when the finality of grief really hits you.

But life goes on, and after lots of thought, you may decide to take over a spouse's role. You may assume control of a business, for example, or run for your deceased spouse's seat on the school board. Another option is to test the new role before accepting it. Set a time limit, try out the role, and evaluate your experience. If the role makes you feel uncomfortable or stressed, you may cross it off your list.

Becoming a hospice volunteer may be one of your new roles. My home town of Rochester, Minnesota has an active group of hospice volunteers and I've spoken to them several times. Most of these volunteers donate their time in memory of a loved one. Volunteering is their way of making something good from grief. Being a hospice volunteer can be painful, yet these volunteers willingly accept pain to help others.

I have a new role, Friends of the Rochester Public Library board member, and really enjoy it. The board meets monthly and I serve on the Book Sales Committee in memory of my brother. He loved books and working in the book store reminds me of our childhood trips to the library. Each of us would check out dozens of books. Carrying our wobbling towers of books home was difficult, but we managed to do it. My love of books started then and continues to this day.

What new roles could you choose? Which ones will move you forward on the recovery path? Losing a loved one changes more than your roles; it changes your life. Though you have the same talents, education, and expertise you always had, you're not the person you were yesterday. You're a new person, coping with grief, and trying to find your way. Knowing the road ahead will help you avoid recovery potholes.

2.

THE IMPACT OF ONE LOSS AND MANY

When a loved one dies, sorrow seeps into your life and
soul. The Grief Watch website says grief has physical, emotional,
social, and behavioral symptoms. Some symptoms are more
bothersome than others. You may have trouble sleeping, for
example, and think you will never get a decent night's sleep
again. Sleep problems are just one physical symptom of loss.

PHYSICAL SYMPTOMS

Other physical symptoms include hyperactivity or less
activity, appetite changes, weight loss or gain, fatigue, lots of
crying, shortness of breath, and a tight feeling in your throat.
Shopping became a problem for me because I never knew when
the tight feeling in my throat would turn into tears, or when the
tears would turn into sobs. Believe me, when you start sobbing

in a store, most people back away.

Losing a loved one makes you think about your own demise. You may worry about every little twinge and ache. Self-worry is another burden, the kind of burden that keeps you awake at night. Judy Tatelbaum, author of *The Courage to Grieve: Creative Living, Recovery, & Growth Through Grief*, thinks mourners may become preoccupied with their health. This preoccupation may become obsession.

You are physically vulnerable right now, maybe even run down after caring for a loved one with chronic illness. See your doctor if you are worried about your health, if existing problems become worse, or if you have new symptoms. Knowing what is happening to your body is better than not knowing.

EMOTIONAL SYMPTOMS

The emotional symptoms of grief include feeling numb, profound sadness, fear, irritability, relief, loneliness, guilt, anxiety, and vulnerability. These symptoms can vary widely. I wondered if I was going crazy. Of course, I was living a crazy life, a cross between senior and teenage living. The fear of going crazy is a normal response to loss.

Brook Noel and Pamela D. Blair, PhD write about this fear in *I Wasn't Ready to Say Goodbye: Surviving, Coping & Healing*

After the Sudden Death of a Loved One. They summarize the fear with one sentence: "I am going crazy and I'm afraid I will stay that way." The authors think this fear can be the result of experiencing sudden loss. I think the fear of going crazy also comes from multiple losses. Some mourners walk around in a fog, others become indifferent, and others postpone their feelings. All of these behaviors are temporary, thank goodness.

Staying in touch with family and friends helped me to see I wasn't going crazy; I was coping with multiple losses. I was comforted by the fact that I have an even personality. It may be wise to see a grief counselor if your emotions swing widely or scare you. See your doctor immediately if you have suicidal thoughts. Help is just a phone call away and you don't have to suffer.

STAGES OF GRIEF

Many grief experts used to think the five stages of grief, identified by Dr. Elisabeth Kubler-Ross in her book, *On Death and Dying*, were rigid. You may be familiar with the stages: denial, anger, bargaining, depression, and acceptance. But according to an article on the Recover from Grief Website, "Kubler-Ross Stages of Grief," she never intended for the stages to be that way. Kubler-Ross "just wanted to help tuck messy emotions into neat packages."

Ideas change and today, some grief experts have added new stages to the original five and think the stages overlap. One article, "The New Grief Stages: Finding Your Way Through the Tasks of Mourning," describes three new stages: shock, suffering, and recovery. You may be in acute shock if you have suffered a sudden or traumatic loss. The acute stage can last for months. You may as well surrender to it, the article advises, and let your grief take you "where you need to be."

Emotional pain doesn't end with recovery, unfortunately, and the pain lingers on. As time passes, you learn to live with this pain.

No matter where you are in your grief journey, you need to stay in touch with your feelings. This requires total honesty. If you're angry, say so. If you're exhausted, say so. If you're overwhelmed, say so. If you're sad, say so. If you don't know how you feel, say so. Honesty helps others to help you and keeps you on the recovery path. Slowly, slowly, you are healing.

Bettyclare Moffatt writes about healing from grief in her book, *Soulwork: Clearing the Mind, Opening the Heart, Replenishing the Spirit*. Though we focus our energy on surviving and functioning, Moffatt says we may push our feelings away, deny them, or even bury them. "The places where we once flourished fall into ruin," she writes. With patience and grief work, however, you can get past the ruins to a new life.

ANGER

A common belief is that bereaved people get angry. Some survivors are angry at the deceased because he or she has left them alone, miserable, and unable to cope. Vamik D. Volkan, MD and Elizabeth Zintl address the anger issue in their book, *Life After Loss: The Lessons of Grief.* "We rarely acknowledge how mad we are at someone who died or left us," they write. Many bereaved people project their anger on the medical team, or the funeral director, or their divorce lawyer.

I know people who, after the death of a loved one, became angry, seething, miserable individuals and stayed that way. While most mourners get angry, I'm not one of them. I never became angry at God, at a Higher Power, or at life. Some of the things people said made me angry, however. If I hear the sentence, "God doesn't give us more than we can handle," one more time I may scream. The last time someone said this to me I replied, "Well, I'd be willing to debate that."

Five years have passed since the multiple losses occurred, and I have not gotten angry. That doesn't mean your anger isn't well-founded or genuine. If anger is an issue for you, something that haunts you in quiet moments, talk with your doctor or a grief counselor. Disturbing as anger can be, it can also generate energy, and you may as well apply this energy to your new life. Letting anger out will help you find peace.

FORGETFULNESS

Multiple losses made me forgetful. One day, when I was grocery shopping, I put a bag of canned goods in the food bank's donation barrel. Shopping took an hour and, after I paid my bill, I reached in my purse for the car key. No key. I retraced my steps and walked every aisle of the store. No key. I checked the lost and found. No key. My husband would have to come and get me, but he was at a lunch meeting, and I couldn't call him until the meeting ended. I pushed the grocery cart to the coffee sitting area and sat down to wait.

The coffee counter was next to the store entrance. It was 20 below zero and every time the doors opened I shivered. The young woman who was working at the coffee counter shivered too. "Come over here," she called. "There's a heating vent in the ceiling. We can stand under it and get warm." So we stood under the vent, arms raised like two sun worshippers, and basked in the warm air. She even gave me a free cup of cocoa.

For two weeks, I checked the lost and found to see if my key had been returned. One day it was there. Apparently I had tossed the key into the donation barrel along with the food. Standing under a heating vent must be a bonding gesture. When I see the coffee lady she smiles and raises her arms in the air. Now that we are heat-seeking sisters, I raise my arms and smile in return. Other shoppers must think we belong to a weird cult.

Forgetfulness may be a symptom of complicated grief. The normal symptoms of grief fade over time, but the symptoms of complicated grief linger. Some mourners have these symptoms for years. "Complicated Grief," an article on the Mayo Clinic website, says this form of grief is "like being in a chronic, heightened state of mourning." Symptoms range from intense longing for the deceased, to an inability to enjoy life, and not being able to keep up with daily living tasks.

Complicated grief can be debilitating and, if you have felt it for a long time, seek professional help.

SAFETY

The shock of losing two loved ones the same weekend was paralyzing. As you might imagine, we worried about having another car crash. Our solution was to have a buddy system and we always drove together. One of us would be the driver and the other would be the lookout. This system worked well for us and may work for you.

Ask a friend to be your "chauffeur" if you have safety concerns. You also have the option of taking a cab. Friends and neighbors may also be willing to drive you places.

Fixing meals can be a safety issue for the bereaved. A widow forgot a saucepan on the stove. The pot burned dry and set off the fire alarm. The alarm alerted her and she turned off the stove before the pan caught fire. Ask family members or friends to fix meals for you if cooking is a problem. Take-out is another solution to consider.

Grief shakes our sense of security and makes us feel vulnerable. Older adults who already feel vulnerable may feel more vulnerable after a loved one dies. According to an Internet article, "Sudden, Unanticipated Death," our experience with grief leads to a loss of security and self-confidence. But that's not all that happens.

Bereaved people may have feelings of mistrust, shattered beliefs and, and may find it difficult to "reattach to a future," according to the article. Living alone can shake your sense of safety. Install extra locks on doors if you feel unsafe. You may also ask a relative to call you at a specific time each day. These precautions can make you feel safer. Even though I live in a safe neighborhood, when I'm home alone, I keep the doors locked.

MULTIPLE LOSSES

Grieving for multiple losses takes longer than grieving for one. My feelings zoomed up and down like a roller coaster. Finally I realized I was grieving for my loved ones in the order they died. Though I went through the stages of grief, I went through them several times, and in the process, examined my relationship with each family member. I clarified my feelings as well.

The Capital Health Integrated Palliative Services website also deals with the issue in its booklet, "Difficult Grief and Multiple Losses." Friends may find it difficult to understand your multiple losses. That's bad enough, but your support system may have fizzled, the article points out. Multiple losses may also cause you to question your identity.

"Who am I now?" is the question I asked. In some ways I felt like the same person. There were times, however, when I barely recognized myself. Though I'm an independent person, I knew I needed help, and asked for it. Grief experts think it's a good idea to pace your grief. This means you take breaks from it. Other tips include regular meditation, identifying grief themes, creating rituals, creative expression, and a positive outlook.

"Nurture the positive in yourself and your view of life," the guide advises, and I did that every day. Sometimes it was hard to find something positive, yet I managed to do it. My husband and I are really close and multiple losses brought us closer. We see every second of life as a miracle and don't want to waste a single one.

SECONDARY LOSSES

One loss can create dozens of secondary losses. What does the term mean? The National Child Traumatic Stress Network defines the term in its article, "Different Ways to Grieve." Secondary losses are the result of a main loss or death. You may have lost your financial provider (which is really scary), your role, your home, or your friends. Other secondary losses, such as being forced to move, shake the foundation of your life.

Some grief experts think secondary losses can be as painful as the death itself.

My husband and I had dozens of secondary losses and clearing our daughter's house was the worst. We checked on the house right after our former son-in-law died. When we walked in the door, we saw a Christmas tree in the hall, and another tree in the family room. Other rooms were decorated as well. Our granddaughter, who loves Christmas, had caught the holiday spirit early. As I looked around, I was so overcome with sorrow I thought I might collapse.

We walked through the rooms to assess our packing job. Every room was packed with furniture and closets were packed to the ceiling. Clearing the house was going to be a huge task, but it wasn't our only task. Our daughter had been in the process of finishing the lower level and the job had to be finished before we put the house on the market.

Southeastern Minnesota had been hit by a fierce rainstorm and many towns had flooded. Our construction supervisor, then president of his church, thought we might want to donate the contents of the house to flood relief. My husband and I took his suggestion and packed items for moving. It was slow going. We would work for 45 minutes, be overcome with grief, and have to go home.

A year later the job was done. Twenty church volunteers came to load the van. Before the loading began, we gathered together in a prayer circle. After the minister's prayer, the church president gave the volunteers some loading tips. I thanked the volunteers and added, "We're trying to make something good from grief." Beds, mattresses, couches, chairs, mirrors, tables, lamps, shelves, linens, kitchen supplies, television sets, books and other household items were loaded into the van. Three hours later it pulled away.

All traces of our daughter's life – the happy life she shared with her children – were gone.

Secondary losses make your grief worse. "Grief and Loss," an article on the Seniors Information Services website in South Australia, says grief affects our thinking. We may wish we died along with the deceased person, the article notes. This doesn't mean you will act on the thought, but it shows the impact of grief and secondary losses.

REDEFINING YOURSELF

How can you keep your dreams alive? The key, according to Brook Noel and Pamela D. Blair, PhD, authors of *I Wasn't Ready to Say Goodbye: Surviving, Coping & Healing After the Sudden Death of a Loved One*, is to redefine yourself. To do this you, you must sort through memories, issues, relationships, failures, successes and dreams. The good news is that you don't need to do this all at once and may take a gradual approach.

I started with the pieces that make up my life: childhood, strengths, weaknesses, education, marriage, children, extended family, friendships, and dreams. Like a puzzle, when you fit the pieces together, the big picture emerges. When I looked at the big picture, I decided I was doing pretty well. Though I had never raised grandchildren before, I knew I could do it. Experience and age were on my side.

You may want to start with the big picture. Sit in a comfortable chair, turn off the television, take the phone off the hook, turn off your cell phone, and "mine" the depths of your being. Redefining yourself is a slow process. I thought about my family history and the ancestors who came to America to build a new life. Their blood is in my veins and, if they could create a new life, so could I.

Your family history may inspire you. But you may be so overcome with sorrow you can't envision next week, next month, or next year. The future looks gray and blurry.

Not being able to see a future is a stressful experience. This, alone, is enough to make you cry. Crying is one of the best ways to relieve stress. Years ago, I bought a book called *The Language of Tears* by Jeffrey A. Kottler, and I've turned to it many times for comfort. Kottler thinks we have to give ourselves permission to cry and my husband and I did this. We agreed to cry anytime, anywhere, for as long as necessary.

Kottler thinks we need to connect feelings (crying) with our thinking. Tears won't help us, Kottler says, unless we balance them with emotion and the part of your brain that asks challenging questions. Right now, you may have more questions than answers. Still, you can set some goals and start to plan the future you deserve.

RECONCILIATION

Grief reconciliation is something you do alone and at your own pace. Alan J. Wolfelt, PhD, founder and director of the Center for Loss and Life Transition, has identified six "yield signs," or reconciliation needs that mourners encounter during their grief journey. Mourners must yield to these signs in order to heal, according to Wolfelt. The signs, and my comments about them, are listed below.

- **Acknowledge the reality of death**. Four people were missing from my life and that reality hit me with gale force. I kept thinking my daughter and the twins would walk in the door for Sunday dinner as usual. Then the pain would hit me and I was forced to face the truth.
- **Embrace the pain of loss.** This pain brought me to my knees. I knew I was a strong person, but I didn't know if I would survive multiple losses. Time would give me the answer.
- **Remember the person who died.** I had four people to remember and often thought about them during my

grief journey. For me, the memory of a loved one is like a prayer.

- **Develop a new self-identity.** Mourners may develop new confidence in themselves. Grandparent raising grandchildren was part of my new identity and I was determined to give it my best.

- **Search for meaning.** This point became clear in a week. When I sat down at the computer and started writing about loss and grief, I felt it was something I was destined to do. I've written five grief resources and co-authored a sixth.

- **Receive ongoing support from others.** Though I'm an independent person, I knew I needed help and asked for it. Friends and contacts in the medical community were the most helpful.

Reconciliation isn't the same as recovery. For me, reconciliation is acknowledging the pain of loss and deciding to enjoy life again. Deep in my heart, I know I will never recover fully from losing my daughter. Yet I am happy and living a different life. Recovery will come to you, though it may be not what you expected.

Your deceased loved one becomes part of you, or as Dr. Gloria Horsley, one of the founders of *The Compassionate*

Friends, puts it, "Grief becomes part of your history." But it isn't history yet, and you're looking around frantically for support. You need a safety net and you need it now. Stores don't have the net you need, so you will have to make one.

3.

WEAVING YOUR SAFETY NET

If you're like most mourners, you wonder if you will survive this awful time. The deaths of four family members in 2007 were an assault and I had to defend myself. Checking my support system was my first defense move. I thought of my support system as a safety net, a secure place to think, assess, question, and gather strength.

SUPPORT

A support system has many cables: family members, your religious community, close friends, work colleagues and friends, grief support groups, medical support, and social services. The real recovery work begins after the memorial service, the flowers, the cards, and the casseroles. This is when you really need support and, to your dismay, you may find it isn't as strong as you thought. It may not last as long as you wish either.

Bob Deits, MTh writes about support in his book, *Life After Loss: A Practical Guide to Renewing Your Life After Expriencing Major Loss*. He thinks mourners need to find and use a supportive community. We also need to realize our support is temporary. "All too soon the day comes when family members must return to their own lives," Deits writes, "and friends seem too weary of coping with your grief."

People who didn't know us well thought we should be over our multiple losses in a few weeks. I don't mean to imply they were unsympathetic. They were sympathetic, but they didn't know anything about multiple losses or what to say. Many felt compelled to share their sad stories with me, long, rambling stories I could hardly follow. I didn't need any sad stories; I had plenty of my own. While it bothers me to admit this, I resorted to lying, and would look at my watch and say, "Sorry, I have to go. I have an appointment."

I've used this emotional self-defense measure many times. What emotional self-defense measures could you use?

Judy Tatelbaum, author of *The Courage to Grieve: Creative Living, Recovery, & Growth Through Grief*, thinks mourners are creative survivors because they draw upon old coping skills and find new ones. She divides support into two groups, *people* and *other*. The *people* group includes neighbors, health care professionals, your lawyer, insurance agent, and financial advisor. The *other* group includes women's clubs, meditation, and volunteer efforts.

Ask someone who has experienced loss about what helped most and they answer with one word – family. I can't stress the importance of family enough. Were it not for family, my husband and I wouldn't be the happy people we are today. Stress causes some families to fracture. Relatives argue about the will, packing things, and dividing goods. Squabbles bring out the worst in people. Do everything you can to avoid squabbles because they add to your stress, which is already high.

RELIGIOUS/SPIRITUAL BELIEFS

Faith can keep the candle of hope burning. Though you may attend services regularly, faith is something you tend to alone. You weave your religious and spiritual beliefs into your life. Rabbi Harold S. Kushner examines God and the power of faith in his book, ***When Bad Things Happen to Good People***. Humans are different from animals, he explains, and we "live in a world of good and bad."

During our lives we are forced to make hard choices. Many bereaved people wonder why sorrow has come into their lives.

Lost in the pain and confusion of grief, they decide God is punishing them. Kushner doesn't believe this at all. Bad things don't happen for reasons, Kushner continues, they just happen. The miracle of life is that we can give our losses meaning.

Some create non-profit foundations or make quilts from a loved one's garments. You may find other ways to give your loss or losses meaning. Options include joining church committees, donating books to the public library, and knitting caps for newborns. According to Kushner, "The goal of religion should be to help us feel good about ourselves when we have made honest and reasonable, but sometimes painful choices in our lives."

We knew our church was ready and waiting to support us. Our minister visited us at home and we met with her at church several times. The Caring Committee contacted us and offered to provide food. Kind as this offer was, we turned it down because we were so grief-stricken. "We can barely eat an egg," I explained. Still, it was comforting to know the church safety net was available. Multiple losses have made me appreciate my religious community more.

FRIENDS

I am blessed to have a close circle of friends. Some belong to the same clubs and organizations as I do. Others are neighbors or volunteers like me. A small circle of friends rallied to help me and created a "caring basket." The huge, cellophane-wrapped basket, filled with goodies and dozens of gift cards, was delivered just before Christmas.

Using the gift cards took more than a year. The twins took friends to lunch, dinner, the movies, and bowling. Looking back, I realized the cards gave the twins some control over lives that were out of control. I'm still amazed by the love and generosity of my friends. Are you out of touch with your friends? If your answer is negative, call a friend today. Hearing a friend's voice can change your outlook on life.

According to a Swedish proverb, friendship doubles our joy and divides our grief. This proverb describes my friends. They were patient with me and, more important, asked questions that prompted answers. Supportive organizations, such as *The Compassionate Friends*, are a place to speak a child's name, show photos, and share feelings. Your local hospice may have an aftercare program for family members.

SUPPORT GROUP

Joining a support group is one way to manage your grief. These groups are led by trained professionals or volunteers. According to the guide, "Difficult Grief and Multiple Losses," mourners need safety, support, and permission to express their feelings. Support group members will be eager to know what is working for you and what isn't. You may get help from a certified grief counselor or clergy.

Some support groups have an activity program in addition to regular meetings. These activities, which may include going to restaurants and the theater, aren't purely for pleasure. Extra activities lead to new friendships and a new life. I spoke to a widowed person's group recently (affiliated with AARP) and was amazed at the number of restaurants group members had visited. If I need a restaurant review, these are the folks to ask.

How do you find a reliable support group? Martha M. Tousley offers suggestions in her article, "Managing Your Grief." Family and friends may not understand why you want to join a group, but you know why. "Your need to talk about your loss may outlast the willingness of others to listen," Tousley explains. These tips will help you find a group.

- Contact Social Services.
- Check with the public library.
- Look in your phone book for local chapters of national organizations, such as the American Cancer Society.
- Watch for announcements in the newspaper.
- Check local radio and television stations.

- Search the Internet.
- Check with your religious community.

Talk with people who currently belong to a support group. Dr. Joanne Cacciatore tells how these groups work in her article, "Sample Grief Group Session." When you talk with these people, ask about the group's rules, which should include listening, no arguing, confidentiality, mutual respect, and taking turns. "If a group isn't helping you, leave it," she advises. I would also tell the facilitator why you are leaving.

ONLINE SUPPORT

You will find dozens of grief support sites on the Web. To find them, log into the Internet and use the search words, "grief support online." One article, "Online Grief Resources," divides these resources into three groups, static, interactive and general. Static sites post articles for you to read. Interactive sites allow you to write reviews or blog. General sites offer support: poems, quotes, photos, and affirmations. The article also lists the kinds of support that are available, including:

- Bulletin boards (discussion sites);
- Information (maintained by a group or person);
- Memorials (pictures/blurbs of deceased loved ones);
- Individual web pages (usually in memory of a child);

- Email groups (either individual or group);
- Chat rooms.

You subscribe to some email groups and unsubscribe when you feel like it. Today, many bereaved people are posting photos and information about their loved ones on memorial websites, and the trend is growing. These people think the information and photos they post will be in the Ethernet forever. While a few of these sites charge for online memorials, most do not.

GRIEF COUNSELING

If you aren't making progress, grief counseling may be your next step. Don't feel guilty about asking for help. Recognizing the need for help shows you're in touch with reality and yourself. Trusted family members may be able to tell you if you need counseling. To find a counselor, start with the phone book. "Search for a Therapist That Specializes in Grief Counseling," an article cited in the resource list at the back of the book, may also help you.

"Grief can easily turn into depression and it can stay with the person for years, or a lifetime," the article notes. People like me, who have experienced sudden loss, may be especially anxious and depressed. Though our daughter died a sudden and traumatic death, my husband and I didn't get counseling. We had participated in support groups before, studied loss, grief, and bereavement, and were our own mini support group. Remember, our extended family also acted as our support group.

LEARNING AS SUPPORT

Some publishers specialize in grief resources. Their catalogs are usually on line and they may also have their resources on Amazon. Reviews of the books may be posted on Amazon as well. I have a small library of grief resources and, as time passes, my library grows. The books I buy are written by certified grief experts or people like me, who have extensive life experience.

Before I buy a book, I also check the author's biography and the resource list. If there is no list, or if the list contains questionable sources, I put the book back on the shelf. Hospitals and hospices have libraries and you may find helpful resources there. A staff member may be able to recommend titles if you are unable to use these libraries.

I've found many helpful articles on the Internet. Learning about multiple losses has helped me understand my grief journey. There's an old saying that says knowledge is power. I believe it. What's more, I have lived it. Learning more about the grief journey has empowered me and it can empower you. The best thing about learning is that you understand yourself better and that is a blessing.

PERSONAL RESPONSIBILITY

Despite help from a grief counselor, support group, friends, your religious community, and family, when all is said and done, recovery is your responsibility. I will never recover totally from my multiple losses. Instead, I have reconciled myself to them, and created a new life. Therese A. Rando, PhD gives suggestions for resolving grief in her book, *How to Go on Living When Someone You Love Dies.* She tells mourners to make a conscious decision to get through grief.

That's exactly what I did. Death was not going to be the winner, I vowed, life was going to be the winner. This decision had a huge impact on my life. The sooner you decide to help yourself, the brighter life will be. Check your support system. How many people can you count on? Which organizations can provide help? What are your weaknesses and strengths? If there was ever a time to draw upon your strengths, it is now.

4.
UNFORESEEN CHALLENGES

If I had known all of the unforeseen challenges that were ahead of me, I would have given up on myself. The first challenges, choosing a casket and buying a burial plot, were painful beyond words. "I can't believe we're doing this," I remarked to my husband, as we parked in front of the cemetery office. "No parent wants to bury a child."

At the time, we didn't know our former son-in-law would die or that we would be raising our grandchildren. Raising my grandchildren, while grieving for four family members, has been the greatest challenge of my life. I had to stay upbeat for the twins and still process my grief. Though I cried in front of them, I did most of my crying in the shower, after the kids left for school.

DAILY CHALLENGES

Sorting through a loved one's things is a painful challenge for all who mourn. Each item brings back memories and stories. My daughter loved to bake and packing her cake and muffin pans was a sorrowful experience. When I picked up her rolling pin, the same rolling pin she used to make the apple pies she gave us, I wanted go to bed, cover myself with a quilt, and sob for a week. Opening a drawer filled with cookie cutters made me feel the same way.

Thankfully, my brother-in-law and sister-in-law helped with the packing. Your relatives may be willing to help you pack items and deliver things to the Goodwill, the Salvation Army, or local thrift store. You may choose to keep a few selected items and let go of the rest. Storage became a problem for us because we still had some of my mother's furniture, my father-in-law's things, and items we saved for the twins. We put legal papers, tax returns, and letters in cardboard boxes and our home office is filled with them.

Keeping up with teenage appetites was a challenge. Older adults require less food than young people and we had been eating small, low-fat, low-sugar meals. Growing teenagers need lots of food and eat often. I was determined to feed the twins balanced, home-cooked, made-from-scratch meals, and went to the grocery store every other day. "I come in so often I should keep a sleeping bag and toothbrush here," I told a checkout person.

We never knew when the twin's friends would come by. One day my grandson asked me if a friend could come over and "hang." Though I didn't know what hang meant I said, "Sure."

Fifteen minutes later, a tall, lanky young man arrived for dinner. I didn't have enough food for five people, I only had enough for four, so I opened a can of soup. The young man stayed for dinner, stayed overnight, stayed for breakfast, stayed for lunch, and looked like he might stay for another day. As it turned out, he left a few minutes before dinner, but I learned my lesson. From then on, I always kept extra food on hand.

Since Minnesota weather can be sloppy, most visitors take off their shoes before entering a house. I never know when friends are staying overnight, so I've learned to check the shoes at the back door. All of us have small feet and if I see large shoes or ones I don't recognize, I know friends are sleeping in the basement. I love seeing the twin's friends and ask them to come again.

LEGAL CHALLENGES

Legal documents were my husband's biggest challenge.

He was in charge of his father's estate, his mother's estate, our daughter's estate, our grandson's estate, our granddaughter's estate, and our own estate. Minnesota law requires extensive paperwork to safeguard a minor's funds. Finding the financial information and completing one form would take him a week.

Though he had officially retired from practicing medicine, my husband signed a contract to work part-time, just enough hours to keep him connected to his profession. But the paperwork blizzard proved to be too much. When he was offered another contract, my husband turned it down. "You have a new job," I said. "You're an estate manager."

While court appearances weren't a challenge, they were a worry. Every time we went to court our lawyer came with us. She was our daughter's friend, understood the case, and knew our grandchildren. With her advice and caring, we were able to navigate the court system. We would have been lost without her.

Grief expert Bob Deits, MTh, author of *Life After Loss: A Practical Guide to Renewing Your Life After Experiencing Major Loss*, tells mourners to seek legal advice soon, before they make any rash decisions. "I can't begin to tell you the amount of unnecessary grief I have seen people bring on themselves because they acted on their own volatile emotions instead of seeking legal counsel," he writes. Though he wrote this sentence in reference to divorce, the comment applies to grief.

You may not have the money to hire a lawyer. Contact legal aid if you have inadequate funds for legal bills. Social Services may also be able to advise you. Don't use the old shoebox filing system. Keep careful records because you will need them for income, property and estate taxes. Get at least 10 copies of the death certificate because you will need them in the coming weeks.

HEALTH CHALLENGES

You may have a chronic illness, such as arthritis, or been diagnosed with high blood pressure. While health problems aren't inevitable, according to Therese A. Rando, PhD, author of *How to Go On Living When Someone You Love Dies*, you need to pay attention to the ones you have. Ignoring health problems may result in serious harm. This isn't the time to postpone health care.

I had cataracts in both eyes and they were getting worse. Since I couldn't drive at night any more, I decided to have surgery. The cataract in my right eye was removed first and, several weeks later, the cataract in my left eye was removed. After each surgery, I was required to wear an eye shield. Though the twins didn't comment on the shield, they were aware of it.

Personally, I thought the metal shield made look like a space alien, and was glad when I didn't have to wear it any more.

A persistent cough became a problem and I coughed for two months. Though I didn't know it, I was recovering from H1N1. When I walked into my doctor's office, she took one look at me, listened to my hacking, and made an instant diagnosis. "You sound like I used to," she said. "I had H1N1 and was in bed for a week." She gave me two prescriptions and I felt better in a few days.

This brings up the topic of prescribed medication. Do not take any prescribed medication that has expired. Check the dates on the bottles. Ask your doctor for new prescriptions if you need them. Always take medicine, especially an antidepressant, as prescribed. Don't stop taking your medicine without consulting with your doctor.

FINANCIAL CHALLENGES

Finances can be a huge challenge for the bereaved. We planned our course of action with help from our financial advisors and our bank. To save thousands of dollars in interest, we paid off our daughter's mortgage. Tracking down her unpaid bills and financial assets took months. In fact, we're still trying to find some of her assets.

We had other financial challenges: medical/dental insurance for the twins, paying my father-in-law's income taxes, paying our daughter's income taxes, paying off her construction loan, and closing charge accounts. Immediately after our daughter died, I went to a store to close an account. I started to cry when I handed the charge card to the clerk. "Please cancel this account," I sniffled. "My daughter died." The clerk wasn't into the warm fuzzy approach and she didn't blink or offer condolences.

Due to the faltering economy, our daughter's house was on the market for two years. It became a burden for us and the twins. Though the house was empty, we had to pay for electricity, heating, cooling, snow plowing, snow-shoveling, lawn mowing, maintenance, and home owner's insurance. Our daughter's house became a money pit. An empty house can be a temptation and we worried about people breaking into the house and trashing it.

Medical insurance was a shocking challenge. Our daughter's insurance plan refused to pay the bill for her emergency surgery, more than a quarter of a million dollars. The dispute lasted for a year and the medical center threatened to report us to a bill collection agency. I called her employer and talked with a manager, who said the problem would be resolved. Two weeks later, we received another dunning letter. Finally, another manager came to our rescue. "I'll take care of this," she said. She contacted the insurance company and learned payment had been denied because our daughter didn't get prior authorization for surgery.

This decision defies all logic. How could our daughter know she would be severely injured in a car crash and need 20 hours of emergency surgery? What a foolish decision. I wondered if the agent had any medical training at all. As far as I was concerned, this person was unsuited and unqualified for her job. Harassment and worry made our daughter's death even more painful.

DISASTERS

The insurance company agreed to continue the policy on our daughter's house if we checked on it regularly. My husband promised to go there every other day. One day, as he went downstairs to check the basement, he was horrified to find it had flooded. Water was wicking halfway up the walls, the wood floor was buckling, and the molding was coming loose. All of the renovation work we had done was ruined.

Many neighborhood homes had flooded and no renovation companies were available. Every call we made yielded the same response: "We're booked up." The insurance agent recommended an out-of-town company and it agreed to help us. The clean-up crew arrived within hours. They pumped out the water and set industrial fans in all of the rooms to hasten drying.

The flooding surprised us because our daughter had installed a special drainage system around the house and the foundation walls were sealed with water-repellent paint. A plumber came and fixed the problem, which turned out to be a faulty sump pump valve. He tested the valve and said it was working fine. We breathed a sigh of relief and looked forward to sleeping peacefully. But we didn't sleep peacefully. Another deluge hit the city and the basement flooded a second time.

The plumber returned and installed a new sump pump. Though we had ordered new carpet, it hadn't come yet, and the cement floor was visible. Peeking into the family room, I saw a large red painted heart on the floor. I asked the twins about the heart and they said the man our daughter planned to marry had painted it on Valentine's Day, when he was helping her seal the foundation walls.

The painted heart, a symbol of a future that never happened, made me cry. But the heart was also a symbol of love and that gave me hope. We sold the house for less than our daughter paid for it. Everyone was relieved, even the twins. The house had become a silent, sorrowful place and the twins didn't like to go there. "I'm glad it's gone," my granddaughter said. "Now we don't have to worry about it anymore."

Two days later, I had my annual physical exam. A nurse took my blood pressure beforehand and it was 205 (which is dangerous) over something; I can't remember the number. My doctor looked at my chart and asked, "Why is your blood pressure so high?" She knew my story, but I told it again.

Four family members had died, including my daughter, I was caring for two vulnerable teenagers, bill collectors were hounding us, my daughter's house had become a money pit, and the basement had flooded twice. I wondered if locusts were next.

"I heard the basement had flooded," my doctor replied.

"It flooded again," I added.

"It flooded twice?" my doctor asked. I nodded my head and started to cry.

"Oh sweetie," she said sympathetically.

No wonder I had high blood pressure. I had also been playing hide and seek with grief. On some days grief was obvious, taunting me and saying, "Nah, nah." On other days it as less obvious and waited until I let my guard down before it attacked. You may have had similar experiences. That is why you need to take care of yourself.

SELF-CARE

Challenges make self-care more important. Patti Cox writes about self-care in her article, "Finding a Balance: Self Care Quiz." The first question asks if you are using your coping skills. Taking care of your health is the subject of the second question. Regular grief breaks are the subject of the third question. The fourth question deals with stress-reduction techniques: physical activity, prayer, yoga, journaling, and music.

I think the fifth question, which asks if you take breaks from grief, is harder to answer. Before you take a break from grief, you have to realize you need it, and this realization may depend on culture.

Rob Gifford writes about cultural differences in his article, "Grief-Stricken Japanese Reluctant to Open Up." The Japanese are resilient in the face of tragedy and keep their feelings to themselves, Gifford explains. Showing emotions in public is considered shameful. There is a cultural stigma about going to a psychiatrist or grief counselor for help. Self-care is something the Japanese do in private. He quotes the Director of the Grief Counseling Center in Tokyo, Yoshiko Suzuki. "I use the term grief," Suzuki said. "And if I say 'grief' to quite well-educated people, [they say] "What are you talking about?"

Each death is stressful and your stress may last for months.

You need to remember this when the days are hard. You also need to prepare yourself for grief triggers.

GRIEF TRIGGERS

Grief triggers – the date of a loved one's death, his or her birthday, your wedding anniversary – are a recovery challenge. You may dread these dates for weeks. Since I lost four family members, I have many grief triggers. As Mayo Clinic explains in its article, "Grief: Coping with Reminders after a Loss," the reminders of grief can be anywhere.

What can you expect? Mayo Clinic says you may feel sadness, loneliness, and have crying spells. Anger and anxiety may return. You aren't interested in anything and may have trouble eating and sleeping. The solution is to be prepared. "Knowing that you're likely to experience anniversary reactions can help you understand them and even turn them into opportunities for healing," the article notes.

We knew the first anniversary of their mother's death was going to be hard on our grandchildren. It would also be hard on us. Family members were coming to a brief graveside ceremony. How could we make it meaningful for the twins? We created a list of the values their mother lived by and gave a copy to each family member. "Helen's Legacy" was the heading and the list included these values:

- Live your beliefs.
- Family comes first.
- Love and enjoy your children.
- Get an education and keep learning.
- Find an occupation that doesn't seem like work.
- Share with others even if you have little to give.
- Know what's important and what isn't.
- Help others.
- Laugh every day.

Planning helps me cope with grief triggers. I plan things that get me out of the house and out of my thoughts. Having a plan doesn't mean I am immune from all grief triggers. A recent experience with our granddaughter proves this point.

My husband and I drove to Cedar Rapids, Iowa to attend her choir concert. Seeing my granddaughter on stage, dressed in a long black skirt, looking just like her mother, and singing her heart out, brought tears to my eyes. Grief had tiptoed up behind me again and, like a thief in the night, grabbed my peace of mind. I missed our daughter desperately and wished she was at the concert with us. But she wasn't, so I decided to listen twice as hard, once for my daughter, and once for me. This decision calmed me and I was able to enjoy the music.

GRIEF WORK

Grief counselor Phyllis Hansen thinks doing our grief work helps us find hope again. "The struggle to live with reality is our greatest task," she writes in her article, "Is Grief Work?" Each person does the work on their own and you can't avoid it without paying a price, according to Hansen. To help you define grief work, Hansen developed a list of eight tasks, summarized here with extra comments.

1. **Experiencing/processing shock**. The shock of multiple losses is stunning and immediate help is needed.

2. **Identifying and expressing feelings**. Shock and confusion may make it impossible for you to name your feelings immediately.

3. **Facing depression and loneliness**. Depression and loneliness can take over your life. Make sure you get family or professional support.

4. **Dealing with the physical symptoms of stress and distress**. You may want to make a list of symptoms for your doctor.

5. **Getting through your panic**. The panic of grief comes in

two forms, present and future. Real panic may set in when
you realize you face the future alone.

6. **Coping with guilty feelings**. Guilty feelings can be "If
   only" feelings or guilt for happy feelings and experiences.

7. **Working through your hostility and resentment**. This is
   hard to do after a loved one dies. Writing a letter to your
   deceased loved one may help you get past these feelings.

8. **Getting past your weaknesses and returning to usual
   activities.** Getting back to normal, whatever your new
   normal may be, requires courage and grief work.

Humans are resilient and, though you feel vulnerable now,
you have a core of strength inside you. This core may have been
dormant for some time and reactivating it will take work. While
the work is painful, it's worth the pain and effort. Your inner
strength is a springboard to the future.

5.

TAPPING YOUR INNER STRENGTH

"My wacky New York sense of humor may save me," I told
my husband. I made the comment early in our grief journey.
Humor had saved me before and I knew it could save me again.
Surely I would find something to laugh about, even in the midst
of sorrow. You may not believe it now, but you will find things to
laugh about as well. Laughing is fun and it releases tension.

In many ways, I am fortunate to have experienced loss
before. My grief history begins with the death of our Cocker
Spaniel when I was in elementary school. It continues in high
school with the death of my grandmother. Later deaths include
my father, aunt, uncle, college friends, and work colleagues. I
was my mother's family caregiver for nine years and, during this
time, had many bouts of anticipatory grief. Some grief experts
think accepting the pain of anticipated loss shortens post-death

grief. This was true for me. After my mother died, I didn't mourn for her as long as I thought I would, for most of my grieving was already done.

This may be your first loss and you don't know what to expect. When does healing begin? It begins when you forget about your loss for a few seconds. It begins when you have your first belly laugh. It begins when you see the first glimmer of hope. It begins when you can talk about your loved one without sobbing. It begins when you set your first new goal and realize there is a future after all.

ROUTINE/RITUALS

Death changes your daily routine, a major support structure in your life. Sticking to a routine as much as possible will help you. During my grief journey I have spoken with many bereaved people. All found comfort in small tasks, such as washing dishes, making beds, and folding laundry. Why are these tasks comforting? One reason is that you are familiar with them and they don't require concentration. Small tasks also give your mind time to process ideas. The human mind is the ultimate computer and, while you're doing ordinary things, it's running in the background, searching for data and solutions.

Children complain about routines, but they really need

them after a family member or friend dies. We established a routine for our grandchildren. The twins were expected to eat dinner with us. Our daughter had taught the twins how to do laundry and we asked them to continue. Manners were part of our routine, but the twins came to us with good manners. After our first dinner together, they said "Thank you grandma," and they still thank me for every meal.

Elaine Childs Gowell, PhD describes the importance of routine and rituals in her article, "Grief and Grieving: The Importance of Daily Rituals." She thinks rituals help us find meaning in daily activities "if you are willing to slow down enough to realize that you are *in* and *on* the journey rather than hurrying to reach the *end* of the journey."

Brushing your teeth is a daily ritual, according to Gowell, and she divides it into two parts. One is the act of brushing your teeth, and the sensations and feelings that go with it. Two is the symbolism of brushing your teeth. You are respecting your body and taking care of it. The idea of caring may be applied to grief rituals. "How much healthier it would be to do a grief ritual daily, just as you take responsibility for brushing your teeth!" she declares.

Using linking objects – things that connect you with your departed loved one – may become a ritual. These objects are a way of keeping a bond with your loved one. Wearing your mother's necklace or your father's watch may be comforting. At holiday time, I use my mother's cut glass water bottle or butter dish to remind me of her. When I use these things, I feel her presence and her love.

Favorite expressions may also link you to a deceased loved one. My father-in-law had a limited understanding of computers. He could send email when he was in his late 80s, but lost the ability when he was in his 90s. Instead of calling the computer a computer, he called it a *computter,* in honor of his love of golf. This made-up word was dad's way of laughing at himself. I often use his word and every time I do, I smile.

PERSONALITY

Family, culture and experience shape personality. If you tend to avoid problems or wait for others to solve them, you will probably cope with grief this way. If you face problems in a logical and methodical way, you will probably cope with grief this way. I'm an organized person, a list-maker. To help the twins adjust to living with us, I posted a list of house rules on the refrigerator door:

- Change sheets weekly and wash in hot or warm water.
- Clean out the dryer lint trap when you're done.

- Tell us when you're low on clothing, supplies, medications, and money.
- Empty the bathroom waste basket when it's full.
- List all appointments/events on master calendar.
- Keep us informed about your plans.
- Call immediately if your plans change.
- Tell us when we're low on snacks.
- Fill the gas tank when the gauge is ¼ full.
- Let grandma know, a day ahead of time, if you're supposed to bring food to an event.
- Let grandma know, several hours ahead of time, if a friend is coming to dinner and/or sleepover.
- No phone calls, loud music, or drum music after 9 p.m.
- Always remember that we love you and are proud of you.

Getting the twins to wash their sheets weekly was a problem. Talks about cleanliness and sanitation didn't help. Finally, I printed out a giant picture of a bedbug that I found on the Internet, and posted it on my granddaughter's bedroom door. My grandson's bedroom was next to hers and I knew he would see the picture. After that, the twins washed their sheets regularly.

Every so often, I would see the kids reading the list on the refrigerator door. For me, and hopefully for them, the last line was the most important.

What are your personality strengths? Which ones work for you and which ones work against you? Recovering from grief is harder if you are a worrier. Bettyclare Moffatt writes about worriers in *Soulwork: Clearing the Mind, Opening the Heart, Replenishing the Spirit*. She describes these people as worry wolves and avoids them. If she let worry wolves into her mind, Moffatt says she "might as well give up on my creative dream." Her advice: Face your fears, plan ahead, and work through your emotions.

I would add one more piece of advice and that's to avoid toxic people, the ones who always see the glass of life as half full. Worry wolves are toxic people too, and drag you down when you need to be lifted up. During this challenging time, you need people who will throw you a life preserver and hoist you aboard. You need to be with people who celebrate life.

HUMOR

Though you are sad now, staying connected to happiness will help you recover. According to a Mayo Clinic article, "Grief: Coping with Reminders After a Loss," you need to feel a wide range of emotions. Celebrating special times may make you laugh and cry, the article explains. Over the years, I've learned to laugh at myself.

Recently I attended a seminar about using social media. The seminar made me realize I needed to post on social websites more often. I logged into Facebook and posted this message: "Oh, my gosh! While I was volunteering at the public library a new book idea popped into my mind."

Only my hastily typed message had an error, and instead of saying "popped" into my mind, I typed "pooped" into my mind. How could one letter make such a difference? I know how to post on the Internet, but don't know how to correct errors, and something had to be done fast. I logged into Facebook again and typed, "Did I say pooped? Dear God, I've got to get these glasses checked!"

Within seconds, messages were arriving in my email box: "Too funny!" Hilarious!" "I want to read that book!" I've shared this story with friends and strangers and every time I do, the listeners burst out laughing.

We all have funny stories to tell and should tell them. Laughter really is good medicine and releases tension. While your laughter may last for only a few seconds, you have taken a short break from grief. So be on the lookout for laughter and give yourself permission to laugh at this sorrowful time.

SELF-AWARENESS

Understanding yourself helps you recover form loss. You may call this self-awareness or "emotional intelligence," a term coined by Dr. Daniel Goleman. In his book, *Emotional Intelligence: Why it Can Matter More Than IQ*," Goleman explains the basics of the term. He thinks self-awareness involves recognizing strengths and weaknesses "and seeing yourself in a positive but realistic light."

Being self-aware helps you avoid pitfalls. Similarly, a lack of self-awareness can lead you straight to them.

Since I was a small child I've been self-aware. One of the most important things I learned about myself is that I need quiet in each day. Quiet times help me understand events, process them, find solutions, consider options, and plan for the future. These times are also essential to writing. When I don't have enough quiet time I lose my logic trail, get confused, and even upset. That's because I don't "hear" myself.

According to Goleman, self-awareness has health benefits, and reducing stress is one of them. Self-awareness can prevent you from shaking in the wind like a leaf on a branch. I think self-awareness is one of the strongest building blocks of life. Are you self-aware? Nurturing self-awareness is always worth the effort and the joy.

COPING SKILLS

Coping skills are the result of life experience. Thanks to accumulated birthdays, I have good coping skills. Many of these skills came from my mother. Towards the end of her life, when my mother was 90 years old, I commented on her coping skills. You used to cope well," I said, implying that she wasn't doing well at the moment.

"When you get old you get tired," she replied. I didn't understand her answer then, but understand it now. I was my mother's family caregiver for nine years. Nine years of caregiving were a long haul and I didn't realize how exhausted I was until my mother died. It took me a year to regain my energy and optimistic nature.

Learning coping skills continues all through life. You may learn to tell when it's time for a break, for example. My coping skills are pretty basic. I eat balanced meals and rarely snack. Quiet time is part of every day. If I am tired I take a short nap. Each night, I go to bed at the same time and I try to get up in the morning at the same time. When a negative thought comes into my mind, I balance it with a positive thought. I continue to learn about grief, loss and recovery. Finally, I continue to set goals.

Staying aware of other losses in my life is also something I do. Cumulative losses affect your responses to grief.

In its article, "Complicated Grief: Coping and Support,"
Mayo Clinic lists ways to cope with complicated grief. The article
cautions people about turning to overeating (I would also add
anorexia), alcohol, or illicit drugs to cope with grief. It also says
you should stay connected with people you enjoy. "They can
offer support, a shoulder to cry on or a joke to give you a little
boost."

GENDER

American society expects men to be stalwart, controlled,
and above all, not to cry. When and if a man shows emotion,
he may apologize afterwards. Women, on the other hand, are
expected to show emotions, verbalize feelings, and cry any time.
Supposedly, these responses are part of our gender.

According to Therese A. Rando, PhD, author of *How to
Go On Living When Someone You Love Dies*, gender influences
our responses to grief. Men may find it difficult to ask for help,
she points out, and this can lead to conflict. Our society is more
tolerant of females, but women may have difficulty dealing with
their anger. Over time, anger may fester.

Yet gender may be a source of strength. A man that is used
to decision-making may make decisions quickly and without
any doubts. In the Midwest, where I live, the gender lines are

blurring and men are assuming roles that used to belong to women. More men are becoming caregivers, for example, and more women are working in construction.

Experiences with your own gender – club meetings, fishing, walking – can comfort you and, at the same time, reactivate your inner strength. I belong to a women's study club that has existed for more than 125 years. The club members are gentle, patient and understanding. Indeed, this small club became a support group, a weekly infusion of strength.

MEDITATION

Weeks of sitting on the couch, thinking about my life, helped me understand grief, identify solutions, set goals, and take action on them. I'm not into formal meditation. For me, closing my eyes, slowing down my thoughts, and focusing on one idea, such as love, is enough. Other people may approach meditation differently.

Mayo Clinic lists some meditation paths in "Meditation: Take a Stress-Reduction Break Wherever You Are." According to the article, meditation has many benefits and can give you a sense of calm and peace. The purpose of meditation is to clear the mind of clutter and information overload and these benefits continue long after your session is over.

Research findings suggest that meditation may help with anxiety disorders, depression, high blood pressure, sleep problems, and more. But meditation isn't a replacement for medical treatment, Mayo Clinic points out. Before I start writing, I often close my eyes, focus on one thought, and pray for guidance. This act calms me and I open my eyes, look at the bright computer screen, and start working.

Some mourners avoid meditation because they are afraid of the thoughts that may come into their minds. Stillness is what mourners need, a time for reflection and thought. Don't be afraid of meditation, for the person you may meet is you. Start slowly, if you have never meditated before, spend 10 minutes in stillness, and slowly increase the time.

CREATIVITY

Many mourners express their grief with poetry, stories, painting, quilting, knitting, dancing, singing, and acting. These expressions of grief may be ongoing. Vamik D. Volkan, MD and Elizabeth Zintl, in their book *Life After Loss: The Lessons of Grief*, see artistic expression as creative resolution. For these people, grief is a source of inspiration.

"A creative work can represent many aspects of mourning: an expression of the artist's continuing conflict over loss, a creative linking object, an attempt to repair or triumph over grief," they write. Creative expression may be used to assess a lost relationship. I've done lots of assessing and it's been painful.

Some friends thought I would have to give up writing. "You won't have time," one commented, "because you'll be so busy with the twins." I couldn't give up writing. Not writing would feel like another death in the family and it would be mine. But my friend was right about the busy factor, and I wondered how I would find the time to keep writing.

I found the time and writing helped me make sense of my life. But the main reason I write is to help others. Though I don't know your name, face, story, or home town, reaching out to you makes my circle of understanding larger. For me, writing is a form of self-care and it can be self-care for you.

6.

SELF-CARE STEPS

After weeks of caring for yourself, you may be falling
behind. Your plans – eating right, being physically active, getting
eight hours of sleep– are forgotten. There is so much to do and
you're on stress overload. After racing around all day, you just
want to sit on the couch, watch television, and "chill." Weariness
has become your constant companion.

Self-care may become self-neglect. How can you get
back on track? Start with an attitude adjustment. Grief takes
time and you need to allow yourself enough time to find your
way, examine relationships, acknowledge your losses, see the
beginning of a new life, and work towards it. This means some
tasks won't get done and others will. Life is different now, and
you need to accept this reality.

EATING RIGHT

This is a time to monitor your health. The one thing you want to avoid is wearing yourself out. If you're worn out you won't to cope with grief or daily tasks. Eating a variety of foods from the five food groups should be one of the first things on your self-care list. Balanced meals will give you the energy you need for the days ahead.

Grief affects your appetite. After the dual death weekend, my husband and I could barely eat, and we lost five pounds in a week. We slowly worked our way up to complete, balanced meals. Some mourners become over-eaters after loss, eating too much and snacking constantly. These people are self-medicating themselves with food. Other mourners reject food, a dangerous practice that can lead to anorexia.

When you're too rushed to eat a balanced meal, eat a healthy snack: bananas, grapes, melon, carrot and celery sticks, low-fat yogurt, or whole wheat toast with peanut butter. One of the reasons we asked the twins to eat dinner with us was to ensure proper nutrition and a balanced diet. It didn't take long for the twins to identify their favorite meals, such as lemon chicken. I even taught my grandson how to make French bread.

My problem is that I love to cook and am my own best customer. If I make it, I eat it. After the twins moved in with us I fixed larger meals, with a vegetable, a salad, and rolls. The twins ate quickly and I matched their pace unconsciously. As a result, I gained 15 pounds, and am in the process of losing this extra weight. You may have come to this point in your life.

PHYSICAL ACTIVITY

Regular physical activity can help you process grief, according to a Mayo Clinic article, "Exercise and Stress: Get Moving to Combat Stress." It describes regular physical activity as a way to take control of your stress. What does physical activity do for you? According to the article, it pumps up your endorphins, "your brain's feel-good neurotransmitters," it is meditation in motion (I love that description), and improves your mood.

My husband and I had been on a regular walking program. But our new lives, high school schedules, and grief work changed everything. Our walking program sputtered out like a spent candle. This upset me so much I came up with my own fitness program.

It begins with 15 minutes of stretching. I stretch my arms, legs, and torso. Touching my toes without bending my knees is another stretching exercise. Icy sidewalks and snow piles make outdoor walking impossible, so I switched to indoor walking.

I walk around discount stores, grocery store aisles, and city skyways. These efforts had an immediate impact and I could feel my body responding.

As soon as the warm weather returns, my husband and I will resume our outdoor walking program.

Fifteen-to-thirty minutes of physical activity a day help to keep your body and mind in shape. You may join a health club or neighborhood walking group. Organized sports or group exercise, such as water aerobics, may work for you. Some fitness experts think keeping an exercise log is helpful. Others think you should weigh yourself daily. I don't do this because it makes me nervous.

SLEEP AND DREAMS

Sleep is a problem for many mourners. You may have trouble falling asleep, have interrupted sleep, or disturbing dreams. I had a series of dreams about my deceased daughter. They were in color and about her as a baby or a toddler. When I awakened from these dreams, tears were dripping down my face, and it was hard to get back to sleep again.

All of the dreams faded from my mind, except one. In the dream, I'm walking with deceased relatives, my mother, my aunt, who was like a second mother to me, and my older daughter.

We're walking along a curved path by a lake and there are hotels and shops ahead. I'm walking too fast, way ahead of the others, and turn back to join them. I find my mother and my aunt, but not my daughter, and then the dream ends. Other searching dreams have awakened me at night.

I think my subconscious is telling me I will always be searching for my daughter.

My dreams express the finality of loss.

My husband had similar dreams and was upset by them. Both of us dreamed about his father, but most of our dreams are about our daughter. I have never dreamed about my brother, probably because we were estranged for 10 years. This was his decision, not mine, and I have never understood it. Lack of contact with him doubled my grief, and I mourned his death and all of the wasted years.

How sad.

Dreaming about a deceased loved one is normal. You may have searching dreams like mine, with after images and thoughts that keep you awake for hours. Not dreaming about your loved one is also normal, according to Brook Noel and Pamela D. Blair, PhD, authors of *I Wasn't Ready to Say Goodbye: Surviving, Coping & Healing After the Sudden Death of a Loved One*. "Our emotions can be so turbulent during these times that we are cut off from our dream source," they write. To remember your dreams, understand and learn from them, the authors suggest keeping a dream journal.

What can you do if sleep eludes you? Diaphragm breathing may help you to relax. You may try the old counting sheep trick or count numbers. Visualizing a blank television screen may also help you get back to sleep. See your physician if sleep problems continue.

QUIET

When I'm working on a book, I often read my drafts and test sentences aloud. Sometimes I do this when I'm washing dishes. "Who are you talking to?" my husband asks.

"Myself," I answer, "and I'm an interesting person."

Quiet is necessary when you are on a grief journey. You need to spend time alone with an interesting person – you. In the quiet, you are able to hear your thoughts and your soul. But well-meaning visitors may stay too long or insist that you go out. Remember, you are in charge of you and can do what you want. As Alan D. Wolfelt, PhD advises in his article, "The Grieving Person's Bill of Rights," you shouldn't "allow others to push you into activities you're not ready for."

There is lots of grief work ahead and, right now, quiet may

be best for you. Thanks to hundreds of quiet hours, I am able to answer the question, "Who am I now?"

You may not be ready to hear this, but you will have to answer this question in order to move forward with life. Learning to live without your loved one is another task. It's a tough one, not something you do in a few weeks or months. Grief has its lessons and you won't recognize them or benefit from them without quiet. I aim for an hour of quiet time per day.

Pat Schweibert, RN, Director of Grief Watch, examines different views of time in her article, "What Does Time Have to do With Grief?" Time is precious and people see it in different ways: standing still, time is up, doing time, wasting time, looking back in time, first times, dinner time, time out, and healing time. A common myth is that time heals grief. But Schweibert thinks time doesn't remove grief entirely. Rather, with the passage of time, our "unanswered questions become easier to live with."

After someone dies, you have so many things to do that you may neglect yourself. This is especially true if you have suffered multiple losses. Having quiet time each day, time to be with yourself and think deeply, can help you survive loss and move forward on the recovery path. Each step is a sign of progress and you need to give yourself credit for it.

I have a different kind of happiness today, yet it is genuine, something to appreciate and savor. One of my affirmations is "Everyone, including me, is worthy of happiness." You are also worthy.

DECISION-MAKING

Grief has a built-in sense of urgency. You want it to end and end immediately. Though your life is out of control, you still have control over some things, and limiting change is one of them. Let's say you realize you will have to move. Instead of moving immediately, you give yourself several months to get organized and find a new place. You give yourself more months to pack things, hire a moving company (or rent a truck) and move.

In short, you think the decision through before you make it. Cutting back on promises and volunteer efforts may be one of your decisions.

Before the family deaths in 2007, I was serving on several committees. One group, a large community task force, met weekly. I didn't attend the meetings for months. Thankfully, the time came when I thought I could participate again and try to resume a normal life. But I needed moral support and asked my husband to come with me. The chair of the task force welcomed me back. "Thank you," I replied. "As you can see, I brought my support system with me."

You shouldn't make any important decisions for a year, according to grief experts. This is wise advice. Your thoughts are jumbled now, and though you believe you're thinking clearly, you may not be. This is a time to avoid impulsive behavior and shopping. Sharon M. Danes, a University of Minnesota Professor, examines decision-making in her article, "Grief and Crisis Decisions." The decision-making process is affected by emotional responses to loss and grief, Danes notes. Emotions are stronger after a disaster, she continues, and you may need to regulate them.

Put on the breaks if you think you are being impulsive. An outside opinion can be an eye-opener. Ask a trusted relative or friend to help you if you are unable to evaluate your behavior. Has this person noticed specific behavior? Are some of them dangerous? Use this information to modify your actions.

Decision-making can be really difficult if your spouse has died and isn't there to help you. "Decision-Making," an article on the Palliative Care Consortium website, tells grieving people to postpone decisions until they are better able to handle them. Some decisions can't be postponed and, in this case, it may be wise to meet with a professional. The article includes some decision-making tips. Identifying your goal comes first. Brainstorming on solutions comes next. Then you figure out the steps you need to take.

After evaluating the information you have gathered, make your decision and follow through.

SELF-COMFORT

I turn to nature constantly for comfort. Our home office looks out on the back yard, which has some oak trees, two Spring Snow apple trees that bloom, but don't have apples, and pine trees. Deer often hide in the wooded area between the houses. I see squirrels, turkeys, pheasants, and once I saw a duck eating grass in the yard.

One winter afternoon, when I was sitting in the family room, lost in my thoughts, I looked out the West windows. The sky was as gray as an old flannel blanket and the trees were laden with snow. Nature's painting was basically gray, until a bright red cardinal landed on a branch. He fluffed his wings for warmth, turned his head, and looked right at me.

We looked at each other for about a minute. I didn't move a muscle. The sight of the red cardinal against the gray sky, the white snow on the tree, brought tears to my eyes. How did he survive in this weather? Where was his mate? Why did he land on the branch at that moment? Several minutes later, the cardinal flew away. I have found comfort in other aspects of nature, but nothing has comforted me as much as the red cardinal in wintertime.

It was if the cardinal was saying, "Everything is going to be all right. You will survive. A new, happy person will emerge from grief." That is exactly what happened. Today, I'm a happy person, living a new life, and I hold the image of the cardinal close to my heart. Nature may comfort you as well.

Katrina Kennison comments on self-comfort in her book, *The Gift of an Ordinary Day*. She used to find satisfaction in juggling roles and being productive. But birthdays and teenage boys and a quest for meaning changed her behavior. She decided she didn't have to push so hard. "Sometimes the best thing we can do is to allow our lives simply to take us where we need to go," she writes.

After she came to this conclusion, Kennison tried to find balance in her life. Finding balance was a challenge, and she realized a thoughtful life isn't a rushed life. This realization was comforting and calming. While Kennison admits she doesn't have all the answers, she understands the beauty of ordinary days and ordinary things.

As she explains, "Real life is just where we are, in this moment, and the only mistake we've made so far has been not to pause long enough or often enough to realize that even this odd in-between time is precious, fleeting, and worthy of our attention."

Chris Rothman, PhD, offers some comforting ideas in his Internet article, "Self Care While Grieving: Comfort Quickies." Some people think self-comfort dishonors the person who has died, but Rothman disagrees. He thinks comfort quickies are sources of nourishment and help you "respond to the stress that comes with grieving." There isn't room for all of his suggestions here, but here are some of the best ones, along with my comments.

- **Instead of a To Do list, make a done list.** I need to have something tangible at the end of the day, clean clothes, or a loaf of bread, or five pages of writing. Just before I go to sleep, I make a mental list of the things I accomplished.

- **Buy a plant and care for it.** I love African violets and have three of them on the kitchen counter. Watching the plants bloom, rest for a while, and bloom again brings me endless pleasure.

- **Make a memory box or collage.** After my mother-in-law died, I made a memory cookbook, featuring some of the best recipes in her recipe boxes. I made a cookbook for each family and they have become treasures.

- **Continue to do the things you are good at.** This could be singing, quilting, or baking. I followed this recommendation and it has helped me greatly.

What comforts you? Think of as many ways as possible and do them, one-by-one. A new friend may also comfort you.

A BREAK FROM GRIEF

Taking a break from grief may also be comforting. Two years after the "year of death," my husband went to a medical meeting in Los Angeles. We had been going to this meeting for decades and looked forward to seeing our friends. Though we loved having the kids with us, we needed a break, and maybe they needed a break from us too.

While we were gone, the twins stayed with friends. They were happy with this arrangement and safe.

The hotel was lovely and being in the company of friends was as comforting as we anticipated. One morning I went down to the lobby kiosk to get a cup of coffee. A woman cut ahead of me in line, realized her error, and apologized. I told her not to worry about it, and that her mistake didn't bother me. "Can I buy you a cup of coffee?" she asked.

"Sure," I replied. Then, impulsively, I told her about losing four family members and raising our grandchildren. I told the story quickly, in only four sentences, and her jaw dropped lower with each one. She asked for my business card and I gave her one. As she picked up her coffee she turned and looked me in the eyes. "I believe everything happens for a reason," she began, "and I believe I was supposed to meet you today."

Her comment surprised and touched me. Since we took our break from grief I have thought about it many times. In some ways, I'm haunted by her comment. What challenges was she facing? How did my story relate to hers? Would she be okay? Grief counselors ask their clients to verbalize their grief, to let it out and talk it out. I encourage you to share your story.

You may be reluctant to do this because you think you will break down. While you are telling your story, you control the facts, the words, and the pace. Though you think your emotions are under control, they may not be.

A year after my mother died I talked to a group of nuns about anticipatory grief. My presentation ended with a quote from my mother: "I think I lived my life at the best time." I amplified the quote with questions. What if we all thought we were living our lives at the best time? How would this idea change our lives? Then I started to cry. The next day I met the person who invited me to speak. "I'm sorry I cried," I began.

"Don't be sorry!" she exclaimed. "The nuns loved your talk

and your tears made it real." Every mourner has a story to tell. Sharing the story of your loss is a way to affirm your life and yourself.

7.
AFFIRMING YOURSELF

Grief is a mysterious experience. You grapple with the mystery of death and the new mystery of your identity. One widow encountered many obstacles when she tried to collect her husband's benefits from his company. Month after month, as the fight continued, she realized her personality was changing.

"This is making me a hard person," she said. "I hope I'm not that way forever."

Grief is a transforming experience and it may transform you. To grow from grief, however, you need to learn more about yourself. Journaling is one of the best ways to do this. You may be surprised by your journal entries. Feelings you didn't know you felt appear and your word choices may also be surprising. Slowly, as the pages of your journal accumulate, your new identity becomes clearer.

Grief is a learning experience. Many people have asked me if I keep journals. I don't, at least, not in the ordinary sense of the word. All of my books and articles are really journals. My writing includes many real-life stories and I add research findings to explain or support them. Writing has helped me survive multiple losses, create a new sense of self, and create a new life.

JOURNALING

In her book, **_Journal to the Self: Twenty-Two Paths to Personal Growth_**, Kathleen Adams, MA describes journaling as her 79 cent therapist. Journaling helps us understand the contrasts of life, Adams says. "Your journal will log your joy just as faithfully as your pain, your laughter with as much expression as your tears, your triumphs in as much detail as your tragedies." she writes. I couldn't agree with her more.

Christina Baldwin, another avid journalist, describes her relationship with her journal in her book, **_One to One: Self-Understanding Through Journal Writing_**. While journal-writing can boost your self-esteem, Baldwin thinks it can also make you uncomfortable. Fortunately, journaling is self-guided and Baldwin says it will reveal things when you are ready to know them.

"Writing for self-awareness implies the ability to increase

awareness," she explains, "and means living on the edge of your current insight . . ."

Keeping a journal has many benefits. Identifying problems is one of them and, as time passes, you start to see the scope of your grief. Seeing a future may be the best benefit of all.

Writer Katrina Kenison, author of *The Gift of an Ordinary Day*, has kept journals for years. At the end of each year, she put the journal away, and forgot about it. Years later, when she started to read some of her journals, she was amazed. "My journals tell a story that I never bothered to read. Now, I see that my soul has been hard at work in those pages, writing the journey that brought us here." The word *here* refers to a new community and house for Kenison's family.

She thinks her journals were telling her she needed to make changes in her life.

Unlike a diary, which requires *daily* entries, a journal requires *regular* entries only. For example, you may make an entry the first week of the month, wait two weeks, and make another entry. Where can you keep your journal? Use a blank book, spiral-bound notebook, or computer. Be sure to print out your entries if you use a computer. Though journaling software is available, you don't really need it. A pencil and paper are all you need.

For some, privacy is a journaling issue. If it is an issue for you, write PRIVATE in big letters on the front page of your journal. You may lock your journal in a drawer or file cabinet. Journals are part of your family history and you may want to store them in a safe deposit box for future generations.

AFFIRMATION-WRITING

As I was writing my way through grief, I realized my work contained many positive sentences. This discovery led me to affirmation-writing. What is an affirmation? The dictionary defines *affirm* as a positive statement. An affirmation is defined as the act of affirming. You may have arrived at a point in your grief journey when you feel it's time to affirm you.

There are many advantages to affirmation-writing. It's faster than journaling, for one thing, and that is a plus. Instead of entering paragraphs in a journal, you are jotting down a sentence or two, something that takes only a minute. Affirmation-writing forces you to think positively. Your affirmations don't have to be in writing; you may write them in your mind. One affirmation can change your day.

My first affirmations were written in the future tense and included words such as *shall*. Current affirmations are written in the present tense. It took me a year to realize this and I finally wrote a book of affirmations. Some of my favorites:

- Down days don't defeat me; they are an opportunity to feel better tomorrow.
- Loneliness is not my enemy; it is an opportunity to explore myself.
- When I think of sorrow, I think of it as a sacred place.
- Instead of pain leading me, I lead the pain.
- My new life is what I make it.

Write an affirmation now. Even if it is only, "I can write affirmations," you have started the process. Affirmation-writing helps you cope with the pain of loss and nudges you forward on the recovery path. After you have written affirmations for a while you may wish to share them with others.

A friend called me one evening. Though her husband died three years ago, her grief was still raw, and she felt stuck in place. Life seemed to be passing her by. Finally, she joined a support group and began to write affirmations. She read some of her affirmations to me and I could tell, by the quiver in her voice, she had started to cry. "Those are my affirmations," she declared.

"Good for you," I said. "You have taken control of your life again."

"I have," she said with surprise.

One-sentence affirmations work best because they are easy

to remember. Before you leave in the morning, you may choose an affirmation for the day and remember it. You may wish to write longer affirmations and that's fine. Write your affirmations in a pocket notebook, on index cards, or the computer. Affirmations may even be written on scrap paper.

INSPIRING QUOTES

I continue to write affirmations and they come to me at odd times. After I finished the affirmations book I compiled a book of quotes. My original goal was to inspire women. When I finished the book, however, I realized it could also empower women. Every quote was chosen to keep women moving forward on the recovery path.

As with the affirmations, I have some favorite quotes. This from Louis L'Amour: "There will be a time when you believe everything is finished. That will be the beginning." This from Wynton Marsalis: "The soul gives us resilience – an essential quality since we constantly have to rebound from hardship." This from Cicero: "There is no grief which time does not lessen and soften."

Newspapers and magazine articles are filled with quotes. You may also hear memorable quotes on television. If you need a "secret pal" during the day, write a quote on a small piece of paper, and stick it in your pocket. Read the quote when sorrow catches you unawares. Share the quote with friends and colleagues if you wish.

EMOTIONAL TUNE-UP

Multiple losses in 2007 robbed me of happiness. My negative outlook on life filtered my thoughts, sights, and actions. Looking at the world through a dark filter ruined many days. Thankfully, the human mind has the power to switch thoughts. You can talk to yourself and give yourself an emotional tune-up.

Dr. Normal Vincent Peal, the pastor of Marble Collegiate Church in New York City for 52 years, described this approach in his best-selling book, *The Power of Positive Thinking*. His book helped people see they could control their thinking. "If you paint in your mind a picture of bright and happy expectations, you put yourself into a condition conducive to your goal," he writes.

Dr. David D. Burns explores thinking in his book, *Feeling Good: The New Mood Therapy*. There is a difference between sadness and depression, according to Burns. Sadness is a normal emotion created by a negative event. Depression is an illness that "always results from thoughts that are distorted in some way." We feel the way we think, Burns continues, and our thoughts are an interpretation of actual events. These thoughts are called "internal dialogue." Feelings, on the other hand, are created by thoughts which are <u>not</u> actual events.

Negative thinking can become automatic and that started to happen to me. I couldn't let negative thoughts take over my life. When a negative thought came to mind, I thought of a positive one to balance it. This was a challenge in the early stages of grief. As I walked the recovery path, however, the process became easier. Today, I intuitively balance negative thoughts with positive ones.

This mental exercise is a form of emotional self-defense. Try it when you're feeling blue. Tuning up a car requires special equipment, but an emotional tune-up requires no equipment other than willpower. You may a conscious decision to think positively. It's easy to forget about willpower when you're grieving, yet you still have it, and may empower yourself.

Judith R. Bernstein, PhD describes empowerment in her book, ***When a Bough Breaks: Forever After the Death of a Son or Daughter***. After the death of a child, some parents don't face their fears courageously. "They rail and scream and die a thousand deaths each day, with each reminder, with every picture, or song, or holiday," she writes.

I didn't want this for myself and you don't either. So if you haven't sat down and had a serious talk with yourself, do it now. Empowerment is a better choice than helplessness. Stand up for yourself and keep saying, "I am a strong person and will get through this." My self-talk went something like this:

- Past grief experience helps me with present grief.

- I have good coping skills and am using them.

- Grief is making me a stronger person.

- Caring for the twins is my new life mission.

- There is more living to be done.

This self-talk turned out to be true because I made it so. I didn't give up on myself and continued to do my grief work. Please don't give up on yourself. Do your grief work and give it your best. Your grief work changes during the grief journey and it is work you do in addition to your occupation.

WORK

Many mourners try to escape the pain of grief by becoming workaholics. They tell themselves the extra work is necessary when, in fact, it is not. You may work extra hours and not escape the pain of loss. Still, work may be a refuge. I wouldn't have survived multiple losses without returning to work. Writing kept me engaged in life and was easy for me because I'm my own boss, determine the work load, and set my own hours.

Rabbi Harold S. Kushner, in his book **When Bad Things Happen to Good People**, says we must view tragedy in context. When tragedy strikes, we focus on the tragedy only, Kushner explains. But if we step back we are able to see the meaning of tragedy more clearly. Only with time and distance can we see the tragedy in the context of a whole life and a whole world.

My friend Elaine saw a different world as her husband succumbed to cancer. He was ill for many months and Elaine, a medical researcher, continued to work. Her husband died and after Elaine had attended to funeral arrangements and burial, she returned to work. While she misses her husband more each day, she has "experienced happiness and meaningfulness" since her husband's death. She attributes these feelings to her family, the birth of a grandchild, and friends. But she has some concerns about work and wonders if it has kept her from thinking too much about her loss.

Though work has kept her from despair, she wonders if she is using work to escape the pain of loss. She also has some ambivalent feelings about her demanding job, which is becoming more demanding.

How do you return to work? Grief expert Helen Fitzgerald addresses this question in an American Hospice Foundation website article, "The Bereaved Employee: Returning to Work."

Before you go back to work, you should let colleagues know what happened, she advises. Meet some friends beforehand to get past the "I'm so sorry" comments. Meet regularly with your supervisor, manager, or team leader. While it's important to tell your story, Fitzgerald cautions about doing it too often or too emotionally. Stop immediately if people start to look bored.

"Don't forget to thank those who help you," Fitzgerald concludes.

Even with the best of plans, your return to work may not go smoothly. Co-workers may withdraw from you, Sherry Russell explains in her article, "Workplace Grief." Since you may not be as efficient as you were before, co-workers may have to take on some of your work. You may be easily distracted as well. Developing a "new normal" for your life will take time. With patience, understanding, and education, it will happen.

8.

THE HAPPINESS CHOICE

Philosophers, religious leaders, and grief experts say happiness is a choice. It's a hard choice. Events and feelings can lead you astray. You may find yourself chasing happiness and not catch up with it. During my grief journey, happiness came and went like a summer breeze on a hot day, and I found myself thinking, "Come back! Come back!"

Yet I knew happiness was within reach and depression would give way to optimism. Bettyclare Moffatt writes about moving from depression to happiness in her book, *Soulwork: Clearing the Mind, Opening the Heart, Replenishing the Spirit*. Happiness requires a shift of energy, letting go of emotional burdens, and getting go of pain. Instead of letting negative energy use us, Moffatt says we can reverse this energy, use it to become "shape-shifters," and transform our lives.

At the end of the day, we are the ones who transform ourselves. Moffatt thinks this transformation requires courage, creativity, curiosity, willingness, and trust. But it's hard to trust after experiencing so much pain. Are you willing to take a chance on life? The answer may depend on your level of unhappiness. Like my friend who started to write affirmations, you may awaken one day, and realize you must rescue yourself.

THE HAPPINESS GOAL

Finding happiness is the subject of many new books. His Holiness, the Daili Lama, spiritual leader of the Buddhist faith, is writing a series of five books on the topic, including *The Art of Happiness* and *The Art of Happiness in a Troubled World*. This series, written with Phoenix, Arizona psychiatrist Dr. Howard Cutler, explores the definition of happiness and how to achieve it.

The Daili Lama believes happiness is the purpose of life. Some of his quotes about happiness are posted on his website. One quote: "Happiness can be achieved through the systematic training of our hearts and minds, through reshaping our attitudes and outlook." How we respond to suffering depends on the situation, according to the Daili Lama.

Happiness is an attitude and attitude is linked to motivation.

Daniel Goleman addresses attitude in his book, *Emotional Intelligence: Why it Can Matter More than IQ*. The people that believe their failures are due to personal inadequacies lose hope and stop trying, Goleman notes. In contrast, people who credit setbacks and failures to circumstances are more apt to change for the better. This reasoning may be applied to bereavement.

I figured happiness was my responsibility. Clearly, the happiness fairy wasn't going to come to my house, fly in the window on a moonlit night, tap me on the shoulder with her sequined wand, and make me happy. However, I could tilt the happiness odds in my favor by caring for my health and spirit. Much of my happiness is due to my grandchildren. Their trust in me helped to restore my trust in life.

HAPPINESS SOURCES

Everyone defines happiness differently. For my brother, an expert sailor and sailing teacher, happiness meant water – a lake, or bay, or the ocean. When he was in high school, my parents bought him a 12 ½ foot sailboat. He learned how to sail, how to tack, how to coil rope, how to tie knots, and how to take care of a boat. He even sailed across Long Island Sound to Connecticut. Unfortunately, my parents didn't know he had done this and when he didn't come home for dinner, they were upset.

I remember the tension in the car as we drove to Port Washington, on the North Shore of Long Island, where the boat was moored. By now, it was truly dark, and a huge harvest moon was rising over the water. We walked to the end of the dock and scanned the horizon. Suddenly, my mother asked, "Is that Alf?" It was my brother, and the silhouette of his tiny boat was black against the golden moon.

An hour later, my brother approached the dock. "I went to Connecticut," he announced. "I had good wind going over, but hardly any wind coming back, so the return trip took longer." He didn't apologize for frightening my parents out of their wits because sailing and water were second nature to him. During his lifetime, he collected hundreds of sailing books and planned to open a store. His dream of a book store died with him, yet he had the pleasure of finding sailing books in out-of-the-way places and reading them. Every book was a treasure.

"I don't have time to figure out what makes me happy," you may be saying. What better time is there? Unless you figure out what makes you happy (and these things may have changed) time will continue to pass you by and happiness will outrun you. Try to identify the specific things that made you happy in the past and now.

Many things make me happy: my husband, the twins,

writing, cooking, reading, crafts and travel. While these components are still part of my life, I realized I had to pay more attention to them. I also realized I had to get out of my comfort zone. If I could plan a book, surely I could come up with a happiness plan. The points of my plan evolved slowly.

A HAPPINESS PLAN

Serious as it sounds, creating a happiness plan can be a casual experience, something your mind works on in quiet moments and when you are asleep. I edit while I'm asleep and, when I awaken, my mind gives me specific directions: Revise paragraph two, sentence three, of the first chapter. Apparently my mind was working on a happiness plan because it came to mind suddenly. You may find the points of my plan helpful.

1. **Face grief**. Multiple losses don't give you any choice. You either face your grief or allow it to destroy you. I refused to let grief destroy me or my family.

2. **Be patient.** Grief can't be rushed. If you try to rush it, you prolong grief work and the benefits of it. I figured I would get to my goal – happiness – in good time.

3. **Believe in yourself**. Age can be a negative or a positive. Because I am a grandmother, I have an understanding of what I can do, what I can't do, and what I can attempt.

4. **Build on strengths.** Since I was a child I've been an organized person. This trait has helped me with grandparenting and recovery.

5. **Set realistic goals.** It's easy to lose touch with reality when you are stressed. Writing helped me stay in touch with reality. More important, I could see my location on the recovery path and my progress.

6. **Let grief lead you to growth.** Grieving for four family members has made me more grateful for life. In my remaining years, my primary goal is to help others.

7. **Practice positive thinking.** The positive thinking exercise I described earlier really works. I use it constantly and benefit from it.

8. **Create new memories.** Grief took over our lives after our daughter died. I called the twins and asked if they would like to go to Alaska. "I will discuss that with John and get back to you shortly," my granddaughter replied. Was I talking to a corporation? An hour later, she called and screamed, "We would love to go to Alsaka!" The trip is one of the best decisions my husband and I ever made.

Of course, a happiness plan has no guarantees. It doesn't come with a tag that says, "Return if this it doesn't work." However, a happiness plan does come with opportunities and we can make the best of them. Each point of your plan is a chance to be proactive, to stand up for yourself, and move forward in life. Short as you plan may be, it gives you something to anticipate.

REALISTIC GOALS

It's fun to think about unrealistic goals and you may decide to pursue them. Unfortunately these goals may set you up for disappointment and even harm. As you create a new life plan, make sure your goals are attainable. If you have doubts, a trusted relative, friend, or grief counselor may help you with a reality check. How do you go about setting realistic goals?

The Stress Management website uses the acronym SMARTer. S stands for specific. M stands for measurable. A stands for action-oriented. R stands for realistic. T stands for time-based. The small letters, e and r, stand for energizing/ethical and reviewed regularly. Though you don't have to go into this much detail to set goals, the acronym is worth considering.

Setting realistic goals boosts self-confidence and energy. Instead of feeling lost, you now have some direction.

Resuming hobbies may be a realistic goal. "Managing Your Grief," an article on the Grief Healing website, says mourners may want to return to the interests, activities, courses and skills they enjoyed in the past. In recent weeks, you may not have had the time to pursue your hobbies and miss them. "Follow up on at least one of them each week or each month," the article advises.

Writing another grief resource was my top goal. I enjoy every aspect of writing: the "light bulb" moment, refining the idea, doing the research, creating an outline, writing the first draft, editing, editing, editing, and doing the final rewrite. This book is the outcome of my goal.

Each goal needs to have clear action steps, according to the Stress Management website, and you should set a deadline for each goal. Working on one goal at a time is easier than working on several. Jot down a realistic goal on the planning page at the back of the book. You're off to a good start.

GIVE YOURSELF CREDIT

Grief recovery isn't a giant leap; it is a series of baby steps. Small steps that seem insignificant at the time may turn out to be significant. For example, my husband and I felt we were making progress when we ate a balanced meal instead of a nibble here and a nibble there. We also felt we were making progress when we took our first walk.

After weeks of going everywhere together, the day came when we thought we could drive independently. This decision was an indication of the progress and the grief work we had done.

You may want to create a time line to track your progress. Write the date of your loved one's death on the left. Write the word recovery on the right. As you make progress, write the action or event on your time line, along with the date. Can you see forward progression? Do you believe you can recover? Are you more interested in life lately?

When I started giving talks about loss, grief and recovery, I made significant progress. I was able to plan the talk, give it without breaking down, and answer questions afterwards. Now I look forward to giving talks because I am making something good from grief and helping others.

Every day will not be a day of progress. Some days you will go backwards on the recovery path. Unhappiness will creep back into your life when you least expect it, and you are forced to make the happiness choice again. You will have times when you feel like you're just putting one foot in front of the other. You are, and in the process, you are healing.

Some bereaved people feel guilty for being happy, according to Ernest H. Rosenbaum, MD and Isadora R. Rosenbaum, MA, and Sabrin Selim, MD. They make this point in their article,

"Grief and Recovery," posted on the Cancer Supportive Care website. "To feel happiness may seem inappropriate, like being a traitor," they write. "Yet it is these interludes of enjoyment that gradually create hope." When you have your first twinges of happiness you may feel guilty and confused.

Other experts think guilt feelings are normal. Though I understand why some people feel guilty, I refused to let guilt ruin my happiness. After all, I worked hard to reach this goal and it was time to enjoy it. It was also time to enjoy my new life. A wise, anonymous person once said, "Being happy doesn't mean everything is perfect. It means that you've decided to look beyond the imperfections." You may look beyond imperfections and find a new life.

9.

A NEW NORMAL, A NEW LIFE

More than five years have passed since my loved ones died. Though I'm pretty much the same person, I feel like the "new and improved" model. I've done things I never thought I would do, taken chances I never thought I would take, shared ideas I never thought I would share. And I'm not finished yet. In fact, I'm just hitting my stride.

Age discrimination is one of the things I face, and it can be subtle or obvious. A new friend, who is getting close to her 65th birthday, has just become aware of this discrimination. "I didn't know it was so bad, or that people make instant judgments about you," she commented. "How do you stand it?" I welcomed her into the older adults club and advised her to continue with her job and hobbies.

Your age can influence and, in some instances, determine, your new life. What does age have to do with grief?

THE AGE FACTOR

When you share your story, people may not understand the depth of your feelings, or think you are "befuddled." We shared our story about the insurance company refusing to pay our daughter's medical bill, and some listeners looked at us in disbelief. I could tell, by their body language, they thought we had gotten the story wrong or missed something.

If you are an older adult, people assume you can handle anything. Again and again I was told, "You're a strong person." I am a strong person, but that didn't take away the pain of multiple losses. Being familiar with loss, however, did help me. I recognized my feelings because I had felt them in years past. Because I recognized these feelings, my coping skills kicked in immediately.

In his book, *Life After Loss: A Practical Guide to Renewing Your Life After Experiencing Major Loss,* author Bob Deits notes that most of the deaths that occur early in our lives are accidental, whereas deaths that occur later in our lives "go with the territory." We all have a history of loss and it may be depicted with a curve. Losses start to bunch together around age 50.

Between ages 70-75 we may experience the death of siblings, death of a spouse, declining health, sense of usefulness, and the loss of independence, according to Deits.

My father-in-law was the last man standing. At age 98 ½ when he died, he had lost his wife, his brother, his sister, most of his cousins, and almost all of his friends. When he learned of another death, he would shake his head and say, "He (or she) was a wonderful person." Then he would go on with his life. Even with family members living in town, he was a lonely person, because everyone in his generation was gone.

NEW LIFE PURPOSE

Creating a new life takes courage. As Judy Tatelbaum says in her book, *The Courage to Grieve: Creative Living, Recovery, & Growth Through Grief,* "In order to survive we must learn to face loss and grief fully and to trust that we can recover and re-create our lives." During my grief journey, I kept bits and pieces of my old life and added new pieces to it.

Writing symbolized the old me and I continued to do it. Multiple losses changed the focus of my writing from caregiving to grief. This new focus surprised me. I surprised myself again when I started to give talks about grief and recovery. Life may surprise you. Your old self can shore you up at this stressful time, and your new self can lead you forward.

What were the best things about your old life? Think about the ones that mean the most and try to keep them. Then get out of your comfort zone and think about possibilities. One of the widows I interviewed said she took field trips on her own, something she never did before. "I just get in the car and go," she said cheerfully. "Sometimes I dance in the kitchen." The image of her dancing in the kitchen brought a smile to my face.

Creating a new life is easier if you understand your purpose, or mission. After three years of searching, my affirmation-writing friend discovered her new purpose was philanthropy. You may keep the same purpose, revise it, or change it completely. Having a new life purpose energizes you and gives you a reason to get up in the morning. It also helps you quell your fears.

RECOVERY

The word recovery isn't an all or nothing word. For some, recovery means the ability to resume the daily tasks of living. For others, it means going back to work. For others, it means going in a totally new direction. Recovery is a process that includes coming to terms with the finality of death and adjusting to a new life. But you never recover fully from loss. That's why grief expert Therese A. Rando puts quotation marks around the word recovery.

All living things die and this reality changes our lives. Rabbi Harold S. Kushner thinks tragedy is an opportunity for growth. Ever since his son Aaron was diagnosed with progeria (premature aging), Kushner knew his son would die. He lived with this fact for years. After Aaron passed away, Kushner changed and, by his own account, became a more sensitive person, a better Rabbi, and a better counselor.

"Knowing our time is limited gives value to the things you do," he writes in his book, ***When Bad Things Happen to Good People***. "It matters that we choose to read a book or visit a sick friend instead of going to the movies, precisely because we don't have the time to do everything."

I already valued my life, but I made some recovery promises early in my grief journey. All of my promises are positive.

- Every person, including me, is worthy of recovery.
- I greet each day with a loving and gentle heart.
- I treasure the love I had for my loved ones.
- When I have negative thoughts, I shift them to positive thoughts.
- No matter how hard it gets, I continue to do my grief work.

- When I need help, I ask for it and accept it.
- Stillness is my thoughtful friend.
- Every so often, I take a break from grief.
- Admitting I'm scared takes courage, and I credit myself for this courage.
- Reconnecting with friends is a top goal.
- I share my grief story in printed and spoken words.
- Nature's miracles are helping me to heal.
- Death has lessons to teach me about life and I'm learning them.
- I'm enjoying the new life I have created.
- Giving to others is part of this life.

You may make promises to yourself. If you haven't thought of any yet, start now. The best promise of all, "I will be happy again." Making these promises shows you believe in yourself. Robert Frost, in his famous poem, "Stopping by Woods on a Snowy Evening," says he has promises to keep. You have promises to keep to your loved one(s) and yourself.

YOUR NEW NORMAL

Your new normal may be waking up alone, eating alone, and doing things alone. A smaller Sunday gathering was my new normal life. The first week after my daughter died, I called my former son-in-law and told him I wasn't up to cooking Sunday dinner. He understood completely, but thought the twins should stick to their routine as much as possible. We agreed they would come for dinner next Sunday.

When the three of them walked in the back door, I was so glad to see them and said so. "But I may cry," I added. We had a quiet dinner at the kitchen table. The tradition of eating Sunday dinner together continued until my former son-in-law died. After the twins moved in with us, eating together became even more important. The kitchen table was a place for family and a place for healing.

You don't adjust to a new normal instantly. It takes time, practice, and courage. Yet it is possible and, like my friend who dances in the kitchen, happiness will dance back into your life. Two years into my grief journey, I had my first belly laugh. "This feels so good," I remember thinking. "This makes me happy."

My new normal includes new writing. Several months ago, I received an email from a dietitian in a nearby town. The subject line of her email read: *Your Expertise and Wisdom are Needed.* Who could resist a lead-in like that? Not me. Her email described the book she wanted to write, a nutrition book for truckers. I replied and gave her some writing tips. The next week I called her and we agreed to meet. At first, I was supposed to be the editor of the book. Because I helped to plan the contents, edited every page, contributed original writing, and came up with marketing ideas, we agreed I was a co-author.

Collaborating on the book has been fun and, best of all, I have a new friend. Working on a book for truckers was a surprise. I'm so into it that when I see a truck, I want to toot the horn, wave, and call, "Hi! It's Harriet and I care about your health."

Trucking terms became part of daily conversation. At breakfast one morning I announced, "I'm firing on all cylinders today." My grandson looked up from his mountainous bowl of cereal.

"You're really into this trucker talk, grandma," he answered. I was going to say something about heading straight down the pike, but that would have been too much. My granddaughter thinks I'm a writing machine, but I'm not. I'm a grandmother who loves what she does.

A new normal may mean a new community. Years ago, an eighth grader in our church was killed by a car. She tried to dash across a street in the dark and didn't make it. The youth group members created a stained glass window in her memory. Though her parents tried hard to create new lives for themselves, living in the same community was so painful they decided to move away.

Moving isn't easy, but it may be something you need to do.

Your job may change as well. After looking at your life, you may decide to get more training to qualify for a promotion. Some people leave their jobs to pursue careers they had dreamed about. Your new normal may mean hobbies, lessons, or joining community groups. My husband and I joined Rotary to expand our circle of friends and interests.

GIVING YOURSELF AWAY

In my experience, giving is one of the best ways to recover from grief. Giving makes me feel good inside and I give away lots of writing – articles, brochures, editing, and mentoring. I also give books to bereaved friends, churches, the local hospice, and community leaders. When I give books away, in a sense, I'm giving myself away. What can you give?

Money may be the first answer that comes to mind. This is a good start, but you have other things to give. Listening is a gift and you may listen to other bereaved people. You may start a support group for those who have suffered a traumatic loss. Your expertise may help a struggling organization to survive. Sharing your story with others may help them survive grief.

Personally, I think giving to others is like a prayer. You hope things will get better and that a single donation can make a difference. Small donations add up at the end of the year.

HOPE

You may have a sense of urgency as you walk the recovery path. This urgency may express itself as nervousness and the desire to finish mourning immediately. Grief needs to end, darn it, and you want it to end now. But healing is a slow process and wishful thinking doesn't change that. If you try to hurry reconciliation and recovery, you may wind up hurting yourself.

This is a time for patience, to let healing progress slowly.

Even with all of my grief work, all the reading I've done about recovery, I have a sense of urgency. It is due to birthdays. As long as my mind works I can keep writing. But I'm in my mid-seventies and wonder how much writing time is left. This leads to questions. What kind of book would I write? How long would the writing take? Who would read it? Do I have title ideas?

Since this is non-productive thinking, I slow my thoughts. Yet urgency can be a source of energy and hope. I can think about books I may write, make general plans, and hope for another sale. In **Emotional Intelligence: Why it Can Matter More Than IQ**, Daniel Goleman writes about the role of hope.

"Having hope means that one will not give in to overwhelming anxiety, a defeatist attitude, or depression in the face of difficult changes or setbacks," he explains.

Hope can be your shield, so fan its tiny, flickering spark as soon as you notice it.

ENDINGS AND BEGINNINGS

Age has taught me that endings are really beginnings. When I lost four family members in 2007, I thought my life was over. I was wrong. My new life is filled with beauty, laughter, meaningful work, and expanding love. Life can still surprise me. Like the nutrition book for truckers, this book came as a surprise, and it almost wrote itself.

As I neared the end of the book I had an unusual experience. I met a friend in the coffee shop, someone I hadn't seen for a while, and we had the same conversation as the one I had with my grocery store friend. Word-for-word, the dialogue was the same. "You look good," he began.

"Well, I uh . . . had my hair streaked," I replied.

"No, it's not that," he answered. "You look happy."

What a strange and wonderful conversation. The happiness I feel inside is evident on the outside, in my facial expressions and body language. At home, I looked in the mirror and compared old me with the new me. I saw a woman with a sparkle in her eyes and renewed purpose. Of course, my age was evident, but it wasn't holding me back, it was nudging me forward.

Happiness is a personal choice, a gift we give to ourselves. Each morning, we have a chance to give ourselves this gift again. I hope you choose happiness for yourself, your family, your friends, and generations to come. Life is a miracle. Today is a new day – your day – and you can make it what you want. Your miracle is waiting.

APPENDIX A: RESOURCES

Adams, Kathleen, MA. *Journal to the Self: Twenty-Two Paths to Personal* **Growth**. New York: Warner Books, 1990, p. 11-12.

AARP. "Guide for New Widows and Widowers," *http://www. aarp.org/relationships/grief-loss/info-2005/newly_widowed.html*

Baldwin, Christina. One to One: Self-Understanding Through Journal Writing. New York: M. Evans and Company, Inc., 1977, p. 57.

Beck, Kristen Brooke. "Life Roles," *www.kristensgude.com/ Happiness/Life_Change/life_roles.asp*

Bernstein, Judith R., PhD. *When a Bough Breaks: Forever After the Death of a Son* **or Daughter**. Kansas City: Andrews McMeel Publishing, p. 83.

Burns, David D., MD. *Feeling Good: The New Mood Therapy*. New York: William Morrow and Company, Inc. 1980, p. 38-39, 205.

Cacciatore, Dr. Joanne. "Sample Grief Group Session." *http://dying.lovetoknow.com/Sample_Grief_Group_Session*

Capital Health Integrated Palliative Care Services. "Difficult Grief and Multiple Losses," *www.cdga.nshealth.ca/patientinformation/nshealthnet/0982.pdf*

Cox, Patti. "Finding a Balance: Self Care Quiz," *http://www.hellogrief.org/finding-a-balance-self-care-quiz/print/*

Danes, Sharon M. *"Grief and Crisis Decisions," http://www.extension.umn.edu/distribution/familydevelopment/00073.html*

Deits, Bob, M.Th. ***Life After Loss: A Practical guide to Renewing Your Life After Experiencing Major Loss.*** Cambridge, MA: Perseus Books Group, 2004, p. 21, 69, 153-154.

Ellis, Roy, Bereavement Coordinator, Capital Health Integrated Palliative Care Services. "Self-Care During Grief and Bereavement," *http://www.cdha.nshealth.ca/default.aspx?=SubPage&centerContent.Id.0=4261&at*

Fitzgerald, Helen, CT. "The Bereaved Employee: Returning to Work," *http://www.americanhospice.org/index.php?option=com_content&task=view&id=56&Itemi*

Gifford, Rob. "Grief-Stricken Japanese Reluctant to Open Up," *http://www.npr.org/2011/03/25/134821398/grief-stricken-japanese-reluctant-to-open-up?ft*

Gippsland Region, Palliative Care Consortium, Australia. *"Grief: Coping with Challenges, Decision-Making,"* *www.gha.net.au/Uploadlibrary/401414769bb03-grief_challenges.pdf*

Goleman, Daniel. *Emotional Intelligence: Why it Can Matter More than IQ.* New York: Bantam Books, 1997, p. 87, 153, 268.

Gowell, Ellaine Childs, PhD. "Grief and Grieving: The Importance of Daily Rituals," *http://www.newtimes.org/issue/0101/grief.htm*

Grief Healing. "Managing Your Grief," *http://.www.griefhealing.com/column-managing-grief.htm*

Grief Net. "Sudden, Unanticipated Death," *http://grief.netfirms. com/suddendeath.html*

Grief Watch. "Symptoms of Grief," *www.griefwatch.com/info/ symptoms-of-grief.htm*

Hansen, Phyllis M., MSW. "Is Grief Work?" *www. sundbergolpinmorturary.com*

Happy Life U. "Happiness Quotes from the Daili Lama," *http:// www.happylifeu.com/DaliLamaHappiness.html*

Kenison, Katrina A. *The Gift of an Ordinary Day*. New York: Grand Central Publishing, 2009, p. 89-90, 207-208,255.

Kottler, Jeffrey A. *The Language of Tears*. San Francisco: Josey-Bass Publishers, 1996, p. 177.

Kushner, Rabbi Harold S. *When Bad Things Happen to Good People*. New York: Random House, 1981, p. 87, 108, 149. 152.

Let's Talk Counseling. "Search for a Therapist that Specializes in Grief Counseling." *http://letstalkcounseling.com/care_topics/care_topic.asp?id=28.*

Marshfield Clinic Education Foundation. "Multiple Roles," *www.marshfieldclinic.org/residents/?page=rwbc_multipleroles*

Mayo Clinic. "Complicated Grief: Symptoms," *www.mayoclinic.com/health/complicated-g,ief/DS01023DSECTION=symptoms.*

Mayo Clinic. "Complicated Grief: Coping and Support," *http://www.mayoclinic.com/health/complicated-grief/DSO0123/DSECTION=coping-and-s*

Mayo Clinic. "Exercise and Stress: Get Moving to Combat Stress," *http://wwwmayoclinic.com/health/exercise-and-stress/SR00036METHOD=print*

Mayo Clinic. "Grief: Coping with Reminders after a Loss," *http://www.mayoclinic.com/health/grief/MH00036/METHOD=print*

Mayo Clinic. "Meditation: Take a Stress-Reduction Break Wherever You Are," *http://www.mayoclinic.com/health/meditation/HQ01070*

Moffatt, Bettyclare. *Soulwork: Clearning the Mind, Opening the Heart, Replenishing the Spirit*. Berkeley, CA: Wildcat Canyon Press, 1994, p. 39-43, 142-143, 166-167.

Myers, Edward. *When Parents Die: A Guide for Adults*. New York: Penguin Books, 1986, p. 24.

Noel, Brook and Blair, Pamela D., Ph.D. *I Wasn't Ready to Say Goodbye: Surviving, Coping & Healing After the Sudden Death of a Loved One*. Milwaukee, WI: Champion Press, LTD, 2000, p. 25-26, 41, 59-60, 73, 79.

O'Boyle, Richard (publisher). "The Successful Survivor: A Widow's Journey," *www.ec-online.net/Knowledge/Articles/widowhood.html*

Positive Thinking Principles website. "Dr. Norman Vincent Peale, *http://www.positive-thinking-principles.com/dr-norman-vincent-peale.html*

Rando, Therese A., Ph.D. *How to Go on Living When Someone You Love Dies*. New York: Bantam Books, 1991, p. 51, 86, 242, 257.

Recover from Grief. "Kubler-Ross Stages of Grief: Compassionate Pioneer in Bereavement Theory," *http://www. recover-from-grief.com/kubler-rose-stages-of-grief.html*

Recover from Grief. "The New Grief Stages: Finding Your Way Through the Tasks of Mourning," *http://www.recover-from-grief. comnew-grief-stages.html*

Rosenbaum, Ernest H., MD, Rosenbaum, Isadora R., MA and Selim, Sabrin, MD. "Grief and Recovery," *http://www. cancersupportivecare.com/grief.html*

Rothman, Chris, PhD., "Self Care While Grieving: Comfort Quickies, *http://www.connect.legacy.com/inspire/page/ show?id=1984035%APage%3A3300*

Russell, Sherry. "Workplace Grief," *http://www.the-bright-side. org/site/thebrightside/content.php?type=1&section_id=718&id=*

Seniors Information Service, Inc., Australia. "Grief and Loss,"
www.seniors.asn.au/centric/health_wellbeing/healthy_mind/
grief_and_loss.jsp

Schweibert, Pat, RN. "What Does Time Have to do With Grief?"
https://www.griefwatch.com

Stress Management. "Have You Heart SMART Goals, Well These
Goals Are SMARTer," *http://www.stress-management-for-peak-*
performance.com/smart-goals.html

Tatelbaum, Judy. *The Courage to Grieve: Creative Living,*
Recovery and Growth Through Grief. New York: Harper & Row,
1980, p. 32, 87-88, 160.

The Art of Happiness website. "The 10th Anniversary Edition:
The Art of Happiness," *http://www.theartofhappiness.com/*

Tousley, Martha M., CNS-BC, FT, DCC. "Managing Your Grief,"
http://www.griefhealing.com/column-managing-grief.htm.

Volkan, Vamik D., MD and Zintl, Elizabeth. *Life After Loss: The Lessons of Grief.* New York: Charles Scribner's Sons, 1993, p. 2, 31, 139.

Wade website. "Online Grief Resources," *http://www.wade.org/online.htm*

Wendt Center for Loss and Healing, The National Child Traumatic Stress Network. "Different Ways to Grieve," *www.wendtcenter.org/grief2/secondary-losses.html.*

Wolfelt, Alan D., PhD. "The Grieving Person's Bill of Rights," *http://www.deloro.org/article08.htm*

Wolfelt, Alan D., PhD. "The Mourner's Six 'Reconciliation Needs,'" *http://www.centerforloss.com/articles.php?file=journey.php*

APPENDIX B: MY NEW LIFE PLAN

Goal 1: _____

_____

_____

Goal 2: _____

_____

_____

Goal 3: _____

_____

_____

Proactive Steps: _____

_____

_____

_____

_____

_____

_____

_____

ABOUT THE AUTHOR

Harriet Hodgson has been an independent journalist for more than 35 years. She is a member of the Association of Health Care Journalists and Association for Death Education and Counseling. The author of 30 books and hundreds of print and Internet articles, Hodgson is a Forum Editor for the *Open to Hope Foundation* website.

All of her writing comes from experience and her recent work focuses on loss, grief, and recovery. A popular speaker, Hodgson has given presentations at Alzheimer's, hospice, and public health conferences. She has appeared on more than 160 radio talk shows, including CBS Radio, and dozens of television stations, including CNN.

Her work is cited in **Who's Who of American Women**, **Who's Who in America**, **World Who's Who of Women**, **Contemporary Authors**, and other directories. Hodgson is a GRG, grandparent raising grandchildren, and lives in Rochester, Minnesota with her husband John and her twin grandchildren. Please visit *www.harriethodgson.com* for more information about this busy author and grandmother.

ALSO BY HARRIET HODGSON

The Spiritual Woman: Quotes to Refresh and Sustain Your Soul, published by Grief Illustrated Press. More than a quote book, this resource contains a discussion of spirituality, information in meditation types, and meditation tips. This collection of 365 quotes, one for each day of the year, will energize you. Every quote is a spark of hope. As you read them, the spirit of woman starts to take shape. By the end of the book this image is virtually complete. Let this collection of quotes – and the spirituality within you – lead you to a rich and fulfilling life.

Writing to Recover: The Journey from Loss and Grief to a New Life, published by Centering Corporation. This concise resource details the author's experience with multiple losses. Contents include Using This Book, Your Writing Place, Writing Tips for You, Writing and Personal Growth, Readings (30 writing samples), Proactive Steps in This Book, Words of Hope, and Grief Support.

Writing to Recover Journal, published by Centering Corporation. This companion resources has one purpose – to keep you writing about loss and grief. Its 100 writing jump-starts will foster writing and brighten your days. This book is a thoughtful gift for anyone who is grieving.

101 Affirmations to Ease Your Grief Journey: Words of Comfort, Words of Hope, published by CreateSpace and available from Amazon. Grief is a stressful, scary experience. You wonder if you'll make it to the next minute, let alone day. How can you lift you spirits? Reading affirmations is one way. This resource includes step-by-step instructions for affirmation-writing and a list of grief support organizations. Think of this book as your grief companion, a gift for yourself and others who mourn.

Smiling Through Your Tears: Anticipating Grief, Lois Krahn, MD, Co-Author, published by CreateSpace and available from Amazon. Anticipatory grief is a feeling of loss before a death or dreaded event occurs. If you're grieving for a sick loved one, a child in danger, a dear friend, a devoted pet, or global terrorism, this book is for you. It is a balm for your wounded soul. The book is filled with Healing Steps, 114 in all, and they lead you to your healing path. Though you can't avoid anticipatory grief, you can get through it, and create a new and meaningful life. Along the way you may find yourself smiling through your tears.

Help! I'm Raising My Grandkids: Grandparents Adapting to Life's Surprises, published by CreateSpace and available from Amazon. In America, 10% of all grandparents are raising their grandchildren. Two acronyms have come from this trend, GRG for grandparents raising grandchildren, and GAP for grandparents as parents. You may be raising your grandchildren, a role you never expected. Each day, you look for ways to make life easier. Well, help has arrived. This engaging resource blends Harriet Hodgson's unbelievable story with research findings and caregiving tips. Though the book came from heartbreak, it is filled with hope, and you may find yourself laughing aloud. At the end, you'll cheer for all the loving grandparents – including you – who are putting grandchildren first.

www.harriethodgson.com

INDEX